Behind

Barbed Wire

and

High Fences

Church of the Brethren Missionaries
Trapped in Japanese Concentration Camp

by

Helen Frances Buehl Angeny

BEHIND BARBED WIRE AND HIGH FENCES

FIRST SUNBURY PRESS EDITION
Printed in the United States of America
January 2012

Trade Paperback ISBN: 978-1-62006-000-1
Mobipocket format (Kindle) ISBN: 978-1- 62006-001-8
ePub format (Nook) ISBN: 978-1-62006-002-5

Published by:
Sunbury Press
Camp Hill, PA
www.sunburypress.com

Camp Hill, Pennsylvania   USA

Prologue

"Your family ate a lot of rice!" my childhood
friend recollected about our family. Yes, I guess we
did--perhaps a remnant of the three years our
parents, Edward and Helen Angeny, spent as
prisoners-of-war in a Japanese concentration camp
during World War II.
This journey began for the soon-to-be newly-
weds in 1937 when they felt God's calling to enter
the mission field and sent the following letters to the
General Mission Board of the Church of the
Brethren:

September 10, 1937

Dear Mr. Bonsack,
 The Rev. Mr. N.H. Zuck, my pastor,
suggested that I write to you as the one in
our denomination to deal with my problem.
With this letter I offer myself for some
definite Christian service in the Church of
the Brethren, hoping you will be able to place
me.
 I am a young man, 23 years of age,
experiencing a definite call into the Lord's
work. With my parents being members of
the church, it seemed natural for me to be
baptized at 10 years of age and to unite with
Bethany Church of the Brethren,
Philadelphia where we are still located. After
graduating from high school, I attended the
Bible institute of Pennsylvania, in Phila.,
where I completed the two year Bible
course... Then I took the one year medical
course at the National Bible Institute, New
York City, given for missionaries. I have just
resigned my position in a hospital which I
have held for the past year, feeling the urge
to enter into some definite Christian work.

For about the last five years I have had such experience as preaching in missions and churches, teaching in Sunday School and Vacation Bible Schools, and summer boy's camp work. For three months last summer I traveled in a male quartet, holding evangelistic services. At present I am a licensed preacher and an assistant Sunday school superintendent.

Would there be an opening anywhere in home mission work or in some small church? I am willing to go anyplace where there is a need, starting immediately.

I am going to be married, September 18, giving another reason for a place to go. My fiancee, a Baptist, is fully in accord with such work. She, too, is a graduate of high school and of the Bible Institute of Pennsylvania. We hope that some day we shall be able to reach the foreign field but desire to labor in the meantime.

Thanking you for your consideration.

Yours in His service,

Edward Angeny

"Teach me to do Thy will: for Thou art my God." Psalms 143:10

This verse has now become what I like to think of as my life verse, for I realize that this is the only way for a Christian to truly know his God and Savior. It is a far cry though from a few years ago when I wanted to live my own life in my own way.

As a child, I was reared in a Christian home, knowing of the Savior as soon as I was able to understand. But I did not accept

Him as my own Savior until I was about eleven years old. Since then, my spiritual growth was slow. But, steadily, I came to rely on Him more and more. There were times when I doubted and was "disobedient to the heavenly vision." Now, because of that and His graciousness, I have stronger convictions and a deeper knowledge of things of Christ than if I had not had these "spiritual growing pains."

I joined church when I was twelve, teaching in Sunday school and active in Young People's Work from the time I was sixteen. It was not until I was eighteen that I felt definitely led to go into actual training for Christian service. I had always been interested in the field of art and of illustrating. It is hard to relinquish these dreams, but how glad I am that I did!

It was at the height of the Depression and I could not ask for funds from my parents. But I did have the Lord to whom to go. I enrolled in the Bible Institute of Pennsylvania on faith and He never failed. It was during this time that through mission study, in prayer groups and hearing returned missionaries that I was gradually convinced of the need on the Foreign Mission Field, and of my responsibility.

Since that time and this, I have struggled against my conscience, my Savior's will and the obvious need. I feared that I would be called to a hard place of service such as China. It was nearing graduation time. All the other students seemed so sure of what they were going to do and where they were going to go. And just at that time when the tumult was most fierce in my heart, a friendship was begun with a young man which three years later culminated in our marriage. His whole life was centered in Christ and China. It was his life, his vision and his love for China, more than any other single factor, that has made me realize that "God's way is the best way" and to trust implicitly the Lord Jesus Christ. As Christ came to a needy world so I should be willing to go to what seems the neediest of all lands, China. Now where I once was fearful, I now count it a joy to go to the "uttermost parts."

Helen Angeny

Edward and Helen Angeny circa 1938.

Married in 1938, it wasn't until September of 1940 when they finally set sail on The Empress of Russia to fulfill their call "to missionary service...in China where there is the greatest need of the Gospel." Little did they anticipate what awaited them during the next few years...

Upon returning to the United States in 1945, the Angeny's planned to continue in the mission field and were ready to serve in Ecuador. However, a physical exam of Helen revealed she had been afflicted with undulant fever-- probably from drinking goat's milk in the concentration camp. So their foreign mission service came to an end but they spent the rest of their lives in ministry in Indiana, Ohio, Michigan and Arizona.

During the years, our family attended numerous gatherings of the 500 civilian prisoners-of-war. These raucous reunions were highlighted by numerous stories which began "Remember when..." There were some tears but much laughter as they relived those uncertain times. Little did they know that they were forming a bond that would be continued even today through their children and grandchildren.

As time went on, we wanted our parents to write about their personal experiences. "Ach! Who's going to want to read about our experiences? Others have written books about it. Just read those," Mom lamented. We endured. When she finally penned the following memoir by long-hand, we were thrilled not only to read about the events but to hear Mom's voice and soul. And thus she began:

This book is lovingly (I think) dedicated to daughters, Carol and Phyllis, who have made my life miserable by nagging, cajoling and covering me with guilt for a number of years to get this completed.

Now at the age of eighty, I have complied. May I now rest in peace!

Helen Frances Buehl Angen
1994

Chapter 1
...a life of plans changing...

The year was 1940. I suppose as each generation faces its future, they feel that it is truly the best of times and the worst of times. Certainly, this was true for us. The agonizing and scarring Depression had started to wane, but there was a war raging in Europe, which had begun in September. As we emerged from the Depression, cautiously optimistic, arguments raged in the United States as to whether or not we should become involved in the war.

The day that Poland was so treacherously invaded, we had arrived in Woodworth, Ohio to begin our first pastorate at the Church of the Brethren. While at the Bethany Seminary the year before, we had been asked by the president, Dr. Bowman, if we would be interested in going to the church's' mission in Shansi Province in North China. Ed had been interested in going to China for some time, so our answer was "Yes!"

Currently, the mission was short workers because Japanese soldiers had recently murdered three missionaries, and dumped their bodies in the town latrine. Deep hurt and shock reverberated throughout the entire Church because the soldiers had come to request medical assistance for someone who was sick. That fateful night, they left the mission, never to be seen again.

Even though we were extremely interested in going to China, a whole year passed before word came that we could obtain our passports and visas, and sail first to Kobe, and to China through the Inland Sea. It was with some trepidation that we considered this, not only because the Japanese already occupied Northern China, but also because of the uncertain political and military conditions world-wide.

It was difficult to leave Woodworth, for we had really started to become acquainted with the community, and felt a strong affection for our congregation. I suppose your first church remains one of your fondest memories throughout the years. In addition, it had also been our

1

first real home since our marriage in 1938 (the two previous years having been spent at a seminary in Chicago). Before going to Ohio we had purchased a second-hand car for sixty-five dollars, no tax. We drove it all that year in Ohio and sold it for twenty-five dollars before we left. It was with no regret that we saw it go, but parting with our first pet, a golden colored cat called Rusty, was much more difficult. During the days in which we packed our trunks, he would lie on each layer of packing. When we emptied the trunk later in Peking, each layer had hair shed from our beloved pet.

Before leaving for China, we went home to Philadelphia to say good-bye to our families, who certainly had concerns and questions about our going. We left from North Philadelphia Station with our family gathered around us. We had decided not to begin the farewells until the train actually arrived at the station, but Ed's sister-in-law, Sarah, started to say goodbye five minutes early, and with the ten minute train delay, we ended up enduring fifteen minutes of sad farewells instead of the quick "So long!" we had hoped for. From Philadelphia we went to Chicago, where we boarded a Canadian Pacific railroad train to Vancouver, and set sail for the Orient.

At the docks very few people watched the sailing of The Empress of Russia, as it was wartime and sailing times were unannounced publicly. (Later in the war, the ship was sunk.) On board they gave us rolls of confetti to throw to those few persons on the docks. It was about the only normal activity connected with our departure. I remember a man caught my streamer and held on to it until the movement of sailing broke it. It was a somber farewell, as many of the passengers had left wartime England and were sailing to join their families and husbands already in Hong Kong, Singapore and Shanghai.

We sailed with other members of our church affiliation: Rolland and Josephine Flory, Bessie Crim, Susie Thomas, and Corda Wertz, as well as the returning Smith family with three of their younger children, all boys. Our ship ploughed through the seas up toward the Aleutian Islands, the shortest route to Kobe, Japan. We were under strict blackout conditions all the way across the Pacific. We also had target practice every day. The crew launched a buoy with a target atop it quite a distance from the ship. We had two cannons aboard, and as we all gathered to watch, the crew handed us wads of cotton to put in our ears to deaden the sound of the firings. Wild cheers erupted when they hit the target, but the sobering and sad reality was that we were readying ourselves to fire at ships filled with other human beings.

From Kobe we were to take a small Japanese ship to Taiku, China. However, halfway across the Pacific (a voyage which took two weeks) a very angry captain placed a notice on the bulletin board, announcing that our ship would only be going to Yokohama, not Kobe--our destination. All of us who had planned to go to Japan were to disembark at Yokohama. The Emperor's ship ahead of us had been accidentally bombed in the Yokohama harbor during Japanese aerial practice. The Japanese apologized, but our captain was so furious that he wanted to get out of Japanese territory as soon as possible. At the expense of the ship's company, we were to go by rail from Yokohama to Kobe. And, so began, for all of us, a life of rapid change in the fluid situation of war, and its resulting suffering.

RMS Empress of Russia

Church of the Brethren missionaries on the Empress of Russia.

Chapter 2
...there are always those people ready...to reach
out in understanding and friendship...

On The Empress there were fellow missionaries from
other denominations, some of whom had been with us for
the week of orientation at Swarthmore College near
Philadelphia. Aboard the Canadian train, we had met a
Chinese doctor educated in the United States. He was to
sail on The Empress as well, but he had to go third class,
in the hold of the ship with the other Orientals because he
was Chinese. We talked to Henry Bucher, a returning
Presbyterian missionary. He indignantly contacted the
Captain, who finally agreed to allow the doctor to join us in
the second class section during the day. So much for race
relations in the middle of the twentieth century...

Having been raised in a town where four denominations
did things cooperatively, pastors and Catholic priests
meeting monthly, the less liberal attitudes of some mission
groups were surprising to us. There was a party of China
Inland Missionaries whom the rest of us invited to a daily
prayer meeting. They accepted, but would then separate
and conduct their own prayers at another time.

I doubt if God sees denominations, boundaries of
countries, language and cultural differences. Christ prayed
that we might be one, and after twenty centuries, we must
still pray that prayer. Religion has had its moments of
human silliness in the practice of faith that has sadly
evolved into great tragedies and shame for all of us. Surely,
the Holocaust had its roots in the Spanish Inquisition.
Even as I write, news is on the television of three cross
burnings in front of Jewish businesses and a synagogue in
Scottsdale, Arizona. Perhaps our awareness is keener as
churches from all over the state came to observe the
Sabbath in the synagogue tonight. But it is still
happening. We must sustain constant vigilance and find
creative ways to erase bigotry.

5

The overland trip to Kobe actually turned out to be a blessing in disguise. Yokohama was absolutely stunning. Every inch of land was perfectly cultivated; a stark contrast to our own country. It was also a subtle reminder of the crowded conditions on the Japanese Islands, one of the main reasons for Japan entering the war.

Frequent stops allowed us the opportunity to be with the Japanese passengers as they boarded the train at each small town. At that time, the Japanese still dressed in beautiful traditional kimonos and wooden clogs, and in the Yokohama station, we were overwhelmed by the clicking of those wooden clogs on the cement floors.

All the English signs had been removed, so we were left to find our way to the correct train on our own. The trains were crowded, but the better to see this mannerly and ceremonious population close at hand, a wonderful bonus for an interrupted trip.

Due to the growing animosity between Japan and the United States, in Yokohama we had the utterly amazing experience of going through the strict and rather suspicious customs system. We had carried our portable typewriter with us, and as we navigated our way through customs we were informed by the clerk that we were required to leave it over night, and pick it up the next morning. I was determined not to leave it, as it had been difficult to save the money to pay for it on our small salary of eighteen dollars a week in Ohio, so I told the clerk that we needed it at the hotel. It took some time, but he finally relinquished it, and I felt quite victorious as I marched off, typewriter in hand. At least I had beaten one bureaucratic system.

We had also carried a large wooden box with us, which Ed had very securely nailed closed. They tried to open it, but after a few futile attempts to loosen the lid, they gave up on that as well.

There was one amusing memory of Bessie Crim at customs. Custom officials had her open her trunk. Lo, and behold, there were layers of carefully packed Kotex. The clerk asked Bessie, "What are these?" Bessie, being a resourceful nurse, answered tersely, "Bandages!" He carefully closed the lid with an amused expression.

6

After making our way through customs, we stayed overnight in a large, beautiful hotel. The next morning we left for Kobe. Once in Kobe, a gracious Japanese woman and several young girls from a Christian church met and guided us to an inn for the night. At this point our group was split up, set to sail at different times during the week. Bessie, Ed, and I were the first to cross the beautifully, calm island-dotted sea to Taiku, a port for Tientsin, China.

The voyage lasted several days. It was a lovely ship with tastefully decorated cabins, filled with mostly Japanese passengers going to Japanese-occupied China. Upon arriving at our cabins, we were amused to find the English-lettered name plates that they had attached to our doors. Bessie Crim's name was printed as CRIME, and our door had the name AGONY (instead of Angeny) on it.

When we opened our cabin door, we were surprised to find a very upset British woman, who asked if she could sleep on the extra bunk in our cabin as she had been assigned a cabin with a Japanese woman. She told us tearfully that she simply could not share a cabin with a Japanese person. She had been in Peking in 1937 when the Japanese had forced their way into the city of Peking. On the battlefield she had tended to the wounded, and after seeing the atrocities committed, had developed an intense hatred of the Japanese. Of course, in the face of her distress, we gave our permission. Fortunately, for our privacy, other arrangements were discreetly made, and we young lovers were alone in a cozy cabin for what proved to be a delightful voyage.

Delicious Japanese food was served. Tea, with paper-thin candied ginger, could be had at all hours of the day. Lounging on the deck as picturesque, pine-studded islands slowly passed by felt like being in a beautiful dream-world, until we passed a ship sailing toward Japan, laden with stacks of small, white boxes on its deck. As we passed the ship, we could feel the sorrow of the Japanese passengers, for inside those stark white boxes were the cremated remains of their soldiers who had died fighting in China. In that moment, some of the passengers looked at us, unable to conceal the animosity that they felt towards us.

7

It was the only time in which we felt any sense of Japanese distaste towards Americans.

One day, as we stopped at the small port of Mogi to refuel, a perilous looking launch came up alongside our boat, huffing and puffing and bellowing smoke out of its entrails. A narrow, standing-room-only space surrounded the engine room. Those of us who wanted to go ashore climbed down a rope ladder, suspended over the ship's side, onto the launch and made it ashore.

Near the docks, there were small businesses and streets which we traversed, gawking like typical tourists. We stopped at one shop, where an elderly lady showed us her products. After being there for a while, she reached out and touched the scalloped edge of my short sleeves and then lifted her own lovely kimono sleeves and smiled at our differences. She was such a vibrant, alive person that I wanted so badly to know her better and be able to communicate in her language. During our later internment, I remembered her and knew that, in spite of rough times, there were always people ready to reach out in understanding and friendship. Indeed, a camp commandant and some of our guards later showed that same warmth, in spite of our being supposed enemies.

I also remember one incident on the ship, which exemplified the treachery of husbands. The ship had a separate room for the tub, which was made of wood. The wood looked porous to me, and I did not want to bathe in it. So instead, I used the wash basins in the room, and took sponge baths. Every morning a crew member came to see if I wanted water drawn for a bath, and every morning he was distressed when I refused.

One morning, while I was sleeping, Ed told him, "Yes, she wants a bath!" Such skullduggery! So as two smiling men observed me, I went obediently to the tub room where I decided, "A pox on them!" and did not get into the tub, but waited a decent amount of time and emerged from the tub room unwashed. As I emerged, there was that Japanese crew member, standing by the door with a silly grin on his face. He had been listening for splashing sounds, and knew that I had flunked cultural exchange 101.

When we disembarked at Taiku, a British missionary, who was acting as treasurer for our church, met and escorted us to the train. There, we found hordes of people awaiting the train bound for Peking. When the train pulled in, everyone surged forward, pushing and shoving. I held back, as I did not think it was a good time for an American to enter into the pushing fray, so our British friend pushed us all forward. Ed and Rollie pushed and shoved, until finally climbing into an open window which turned out to be the restroom. Fortunately, they had also yanked in our hand luggage. I was the last of our group to get aboard. As the train started to pull away, I was hanging onto the steps outside the train. I continued to push, any thoughts of holding back long forgotten. An elderly Chinese gentleman gave his seat to me and the British woman, who had wanted to share our stateroom. The seat was a large, oblong-lidded basket, filled with stale smelling bread he had garnered from a Tientsin hotel. All the way to the exciting, ancient city of Peking, my seat companion regaled me with tales of life in China.

Chapter 3
*The world without the Christmas Story is
indeed a sad and empty place.*

Finally, we reached Peking, centuries old, yet still surrounded by thick, medieval walls. Its walls contained the mysteries of emperors and empresses, concubines, eunuchs, and court plottings since its far distant beginnings. Until recently, only Marco Polo, some Catholic priests, and a handful of others have penetrated, and lived within, its ancient walls. At the center of the city stood the Forbidden City, where rulers held sway and gathered immense tribute and riches from the far reaches of China. Surrounded by its walls, the yellow-tiled-roofed buildings of the Forbidden City glittered and shone in the pale, fall sunlight.

Our language school was located in the Imperial City, just outside the Forbidden City. Here, shops and open market places catered to the teeming population. Jade Street sold jewelry, Embroidery Street sold fabulous silk brocades, satins and embroideries, and Pig Street sold meats. Many of these streets dated back to the time of the Empress Dowager, and many even before that. One store which amused us had a sign that said, "Eye glasses made by the latest Methodist." We never did find that Methodist.

In the Imperial City, individual homes were surrounded by walls, as was our language school. Within our school campus there were several attractive buildings, with classrooms on the lower floor, and student rooms on the two other remaining floors. The students were mostly missionaries from the United States, England and Sweden, representing a variety of denominations. Some diplomats, news reporters and business people, eager to learn Chung quo tsu (the Chinese language), were also enrolled.

In a short time, we were all engrossed in intense language study. The day started with the head teacher, an engaging and excellent instructor nicknamed Dearest, who on the first day began with one word, "I." Every day he enlarged our vocabulary. From there we moved to classes of six to eight students, where we reviewed new vocabulary. Finally, we each went on to private classes, in small cubicles, for one-on-one lessons, reviewing the new words again.

For me, language study was extremely difficult. I still think that one needs to be musical in order to catch the tonal shadings, which give meaning to the Mandarin Chinese. Language seemed to come easily for Ed, and by year's end he could converse in simple sentences with the Chinese in Baguio, a city in the Philippine Islands where we were finally compelled to move our language school.

Tea was served several times a day. Afternoons were free for study and exploration of Peking.

After just a few short weeks, the American students were invited to Dr. John Hayes's home, the capable head of the school. Ostensibly the occasion was a welcoming party for the Americans, but secretly it was to inform us that the State Department had suggested we leave China due to the deepening rancor and tension between Japan and the United States. The necessity of such secrecy was due to the fact that the few Japanese students enrolled at the school were actually informers for their government.

This suggestion was a shock to those of us who had just arrived. Most of our luggage had not even arrived yet. We were all too stunned to know how to react. Since the State Department could only suggest, not demand, that we leave, we decided to wait awhile longer before deciding upon a course of action. In the meantime, tensions continued to mount between Japanese and Westerners in the city, and there was a subtle, yet constant resistance from the Chinese, who were suffering under the Japanese regime.

Things got particularly tense for several weeks after a high ranking Japanese officer was shot and killed by unknown assailants. The Japanese immediately closed all the main gates to the city, allowing only a few smaller gates open through which food stuffs were allowed under close surveillance. An eerie feeling was shared by all as we realized that we were virtually prisoners within the city walls. Rumors abounded, and every evening we gathered around the radio, hoping to hear news from Shanghai, but only to hear static. After awhile tension abated, the gates were re-opened, and life in the ancient city flowed on as it had throughout hundreds of years.

Overall, life was fairly pleasant, structured mainly by our studies. Occasionally, there were parties and lectures given by artists and scientists on the Chinese life and culture to break up the routine, and most of us attended the Union Church. We were also entertained in some of the local missionaries' homes from time to time. Some of these homes were quite luxurious, and there were numerous discussions about what we, as younger missionaries, felt about this, and how we thought it should be handled in the face of the growing poverty. In the outlaying provinces, mission homes were much simpler, but still far superior to the local, average Chinese home. Some felt that we should live as the average person did, while others were concerned that to do so would undermine our health and therefore our capacity to have any time to serve the church.

These tough questions became academic when our Church of the Brethren missions were forced to evacuate Shansi Province. Missionaries from there had arrived in Peking just before Christmas. Prior to our arrival in the fall of 1941, the telegraph lines had been cut between Peking and Shansi, leaving the missionaries completely isolated. One of the men told us that if they could have communicated with the United States, they would have advised us not to come to China.

Other denominations were facing the same problems as well. The people from our church in Shansi, who had been forced to evacuate, were invited to stay in the Methodist compound, until decisions could be made. In the meantime, Christmas was approaching, language study continued, and we were becoming better acquainted with the students and the Chinese people involved in the school.

Our group planned for the Christmas holidays and a birthday party for Rolland Flory, whose birthday happened to fall on Christmas. On Christmas Eve, the school was touched beyond words when fifty children from the Salvation Army came and sang Christmas carols in the moonlit garden of the school. It made us all a bit homesick, but happy, to see all those children, warm in their thickly-padded garments, singing the ancient familiar carols. Even amidst all that joy, we all sensed that drastic changes were about to take place, due to the increasing enmity between Japan and the United States.

Christmas morning, Ed and I were delighted to have been chosen to go to the French bakery to pick up a birthday cake and gift for Rollie from all of us. Since Rolland was an agricultural missionary, we purchased an interesting, potted, and gnarled pine tree and went on down busy Hatamen Street to the bakery.

For me, this was really the first time that the culture shock had hit me. Inside our walled compound, Christmas lights, trees, and decorations abounded. Parties and celebrations were rife. Outside however, it was life as usual. Of course, I knew already this, but actually experiencing it firsthand, gave me a sense of sadness, realizing anew that for all the rest of the non-western world, this was reality. The world without the Christmas story is indeed a sad and empty place.

As I look back on this time in history, I realize how fortunate we were to see Peking as it existed at that time. Even though it was under the cruel regime of Japanese occupation, there was still the feeling of ancient splendor all around us. The impressive twenty-foot thick wall surrounding the city with towers at each gate, the agricultural hall in the nearby countryside with the blue-tiled roof and the scarlet and gold interior wall decorations, and the graceful circular white marble of the temple altar where emperors had worshiped annually for centuries all thrilled our artistic senses. Peking was the center of the universe for the Chinese people. With the blue skies above us, and the wind gently blowing around us, one had the sense that perhaps this was truly so.

Today, this same spot is surrounded by tall buildings and the clutter and hum of a modern city. The ancient walls of the city have been removed, a subway has been built, and Chinese in modern dress fill the streets.

13

However, not all the changes have been negative. Gone too, are the professional beggars, people dying on the streets, unsanitary conditions, rampant hunger, and poor health facilities. When we were there, the Rockefeller Medical Center, built in the style of the Forbidden City with yellow-tiled roofs, gave care to many but faced extreme obstacles in trying to care for all those who needed it. Amidst all this change, one thing remains the same, the ever present fear of the current political regime. Emperors, unstable warlords, Western exploration, the Boxer Rebellion, Chaing Kai Shek and the nationalist government, and now the harsh Communist rule have terrified these people for centuries. Somehow, they have managed to survive, change, and hope just like people the world over. The courage and resourcefulness of the Chinese people has endured throughout the centuries. Bright and personable, they have persisted through famine, floods and turmoil, and we can only pray that brighter, happier days lie ahead for this nation.

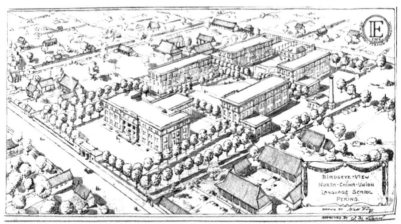

Peking Language School.

Chapter 4
We need exciting, imaginative people...
to bring help to a perishing world.

Fall and winter quickly passed and as the spring of
1941 approached, we knew that our days were numbered
in Northern China. The Chinese, who had any connection
with Westerners, were in danger of persecution by the
Japanese. Therefore, our western missionary community,
which had been ousted from their mission in the interior,
decided it was time to leave.

Most of us wanted to get into free, western China,
which was still under the control of the Nationalists.
Schemes abounded of how this could be accomplished, but
there was one that really stood out. One night at our
apartment, Bill and Jessie Junkin, two Southern
Presbyterians, revealed to us that a Catholic group had
offered to secretly help us go by land to the Chungking
area. (For the most part, missions abroad cooperated with
one another, especially in times of danger, sickness and
schooling for their children, far more than some
denominations at home.) The evening the Junkins came,
we had to discuss our plans in lowered voices for fear of
being overheard. As more details were revealed, we realized
that too many Chinese people would be placing themselves
in harm's way, therefore we declined.

We finally decided to move the Language school to the
Philippine Islands, continue our studies for the remainder
of the year, and then fly into Chungking, China, where our
church had made arrangements to help an Anglican
Canadian with their work. The older missionaries decided
to return to the United States because they could not
return to Shansi in the foreseeable future.

In case anyone thinks that these decisions were arrived
at in peace and harmony as all good sweet Christian
missionaries are supposed to do, you are mistaken!
Someone has said that a bunch of missionary leaders are

15

like a bunch of generals: all set on their pet ideas of how to proceed in a crisis. This conclusion to leave was reached, finally, by consensus but only after some pretty heated discussion.

At the time, the senior missionaries were staying with their children in the Methodist compound. One of them heard a humorous conversation between two young children, whose Methodist parents were also returning to the United States. "Mish kids" always had an adjustment time when returning to the States on furlough. One ten year old boy said to another, "If kids in America make fun of me, I'm going to curse them out, but I'll do it in Chinese so my mother won't lose face!"

A similar tale was told of one of our internee camp children. When he returned with his parents after three years of incarceration by the Japanese, he was asked by a church member how it felt to be the son of a missionary. He candidly replied, "Well, sir, it's not what it's cracked up to be!" I suppose the children of missionaries and other youngsters living abroad still have some of the same feelings today. While exciting and glamorous at times, living in a far away country does take its toll. It is a constant price these parents and children pay for service to their church, business, and country.

In the spring of 1941, our Brethren group left Peking. Some decided to return home, but we decided to sail from Tientsin to Shanghai and then take another ship to the Philippines. We stayed in Tientsin overnight.

That evening a nurse, the wife of a Chinese doctor, came to see us. She had worked at our mission hospital in Shansi. It was too risky for the doctor to come because of the presence of Japanese in the hotel. We met in a very secluded, dimly-lit lounge, and she showed extreme courage in coming. All through our stay in the Orient, there were Chinese, Filipinos, and even some Japanese who took great risks to help Americans.

We sailed the next morning on a British ship. It had a plaque stating that it had been sunk, raised, and refurbished. How comforting... It was cold, and we ran into some pretty rough seas which made almost everyone seasick. As the waves and winds battered us, the end of the ship would rise out of the water, give a hefty shudder and crash back down again. Bessie's cabin was in the stern of the ship, so she really felt the motion. She also had icicles on the walls of her cabin. Throughout the night, we could hear White Russian guards tramp back and forth on the deck above us, guarding against Chinese bandits. The ship had sharp steel blades, like points, along the railings to keep them from boarding in case of an attack.

On arriving in Shanghai, there was a group of Quakers who offered the Brethren group their warm hospitality to stay in their homes. At that time the Quakers and Brethren, two of the historic peace churches, were doing relief work in Shanghai.

The couple that we stayed with had high positions in an oil company and bank, and was not at home when we arrived. The servants greeted us as did a Myna bird at the end of a large entrance hall, saying "Hello there! Hello there!" We were shown to our room and then to a small sitting room, a large, welcoming fire in the fireplace. We appreciated that, as wood was scarce in Shanghai at that time. There were also two affectionate dogs: one, an English bulldog and the other a small terrier.

When the host and hostess finally arrived home that evening, we all gathered in a rather formal dining room to eat. The hostess placed the Myna bird on a large stand next to her at the end of the table. She fed it bits from her plate during dinner. The bulldog sat at the table opposite us, but just as an observer. They suggested that we have a Quaker grace, each person silently praying to themselves. Afterward, they explained that the last missionary they had entertained had said such a long grace that the bulldog got off his chair and paced the room, growling in anguish.

Later, they showed home movies of a formal party they had hosted in their home. Well-dressed Chinese, English and American guests (obviously top society as they named them) moved about and then were seated at the table. Lo and behold, the guest of honor whose birthday they were celebrating sat at the end of the table with a gold paper crown on his head. It was the beloved English bulldog! It looked like something out of Alice in Wonderland, fortunately without the Cheshire cat.

We spent several days in Shanghai, where wealth and poverty lived side by side. Indian sikits--tall and threatening in their turbans--towered over the teeming populace, acting as police.

One day, we were invited to visit a warehouse, in which Jewish refugees from Europe were being housed. The Quakers and Brethren were trying to assist these unfortunate people, caught in a quagmire of senseless Nazi hatred. They had very few possessions. We noticed musical instruments and their few belongings in boxes or suitcases. Housed in double bunks in dark, cheerless surroundings, they stood in food lines, utterly cut off from the world they had known. One middle-aged man filled his empty, expensive briefcase with soup to take back to his wife. These people could have been given refuge in any number of countries, including our own, but the United States had turned them away. Shanghai was the only place that would admit them. Shame engulfed all of us.

Some occasions are so special that they brighten even the darkest of circumstances. One woman in the warehouse had just given birth, and with her new baby in her arms she seemed serene and hopeful, almost unaware of the roughly finished warehouse room.

Little did Jo and I know that within a short time we too would be in almost the same situation. The room that I brought Carol back to after she was born was a former jail room with bars at the small window, in the Igorot barracks at Camp John Hay. I remember coming into the room one day as the sun cast shadows of the bars across Carol's bed. That was a low moment for me. A month later, Josephine gave birth to Jimmy, while Rolland was in the hands of the Japanese secret police. His condition at that time was unknown, informed only of the fact that he had been tortured.

That was over fifty years ago and people the world over have suffered far worse and more horrible fates. Even now, enjoying our comfortable American home, there are thousands of homeless with no medical care or food, and certainly little hope. Since returning home, I have felt our

18

attractive, sometime elegant houses and church buildings are a deep and sinful reproach to our Christian belief. The majority of us are only skimming the surface of need and not working with deep concern and dedication on solving the real problems all around us. Our Christian business men and women, our Christian politicians, the movers and shakers of our communities do proportionately little compared to the need. We need exciting, imaginative people to be our leaders and they simply are not there in the great numbers in which they're needed to bring help to a perishing world.

The night before our ship, The Bernaden de St. Pierre, sailed, Rolland, Jo, Ed and I were advised that we should board the ship that evening when the ship was docked in the Japanese section of Shanghai. It would be closed to traffic if an ugly incident involving the Chinese were to take place, and we would not be allowed to enter that area. All night long the ship was loaded, and none of us got much sleep. The ship was far less elegant than its impressive name. It was a French ship belonging to the Free French. Due to the war, they were not able to keep it in very good repair, but the crew did the best they could to make the voyage comfortable.

One amusing incident took place at a Friday evening dinner. The French waiter gave the four of us the menus. Sirloin steak was listed. Since arriving in China we had not eaten steak, so we ordered them. When we were served, Jo and I were given steaks, but Rollie and Ed were served fish. The waiter explained to them, "this is Friday and you are Fathers." Poor Rollie wasn't a minister but he was lumped in with Ed. Jo and I decided that since we were given the steaks, they were ours, and forced the men to eat fish. We decided the reason for the men being served fish was that their supply of steaks was limited and, of course, the French's love of the ladies.

After several days, we docked in Manila. The cold of Northern China to the tropical heat of Manila was quite a change. We stayed a few days, touring "The Pearl of the Orient." Manila dated back four hundred years. A Lutheran pastor took us to the old walled city, and in a cathedral there he introduced us to several priests, who took us on the tour of this beautiful church. The highlight of the tour was one large room, which was filled with ancient and gorgeously-colored vestments. We were completely awed at the beauty displayed.

We also visited the President's house, an art museum, and attended a concert at the Santo Tomas University. The minister also took us to old Fort Santiago, a prison on the Passig River which had daily tides. Down in one of the dungeons, there were wrist and ankle rings fastened into the stone walls. In the old days when the tide washed in, the river would relentlessly drown the chained prisoners. It was a most forbidding place. The Japanese used the prison during their occupation for Filipinos and Americans alike. We also heard rumors that they used it for their own recalcitrants.

Finally, we boarded a train to Baguio, the summer capital of the Philippines. It was five thousand feet in elevation with an average temperature of seventy degrees, a wonderful place at that time to live and study. The first part of the journey was by train, and about halfway there, we left the train to get on a bus. It was unbelievably crowded inside that trusty old vehicle, and loaded on top of the bus were baskets, chickens, and luggage. In this way we made our way up the zigzag trail, which was built perilously into the side of mountains, through lush countryside. Pine trees began to appear as we ascended.

At first, our Brethren group found two framed houses joined by an entryway. Bessie Crim, Susie Thomas and the Florys lived on one side. Dr. Cunningham, his wife Ellen and their three-year-old son, Larry, and Ed and I shared the other house. We had a joint kitchen. In order for all of us to have time for language study, we hired an Igorot girl to do the cooking. She really did quite well, having been trained at Easter School, an Episcopalian institution.

Each of the women took turns shopping in the open Baguio market. It was colorful and alive with people bargaining and trading. All kinds of seafood, caribou meat, vegetables, wonderful tropical fruit and bunches of flowers were for sale. I especially enjoyed the velvety, creamy white gardenias.

After a while we found less expensive places to live, and we each moved to individual apartments or houses. When we were in our own homes, we did our own cooking. I had an electric hot plate and a small, interesting wooden stove which really worked quite well. The oven had doors on two sides, which was a very good idea because you could put pies and meats in the back, and when they were done you could open the back door and remove them without disturbing the things in front.

Stacked underneath our house was wood, inhabited by large, tropical roaches, at least two inches in length. In the evening these invaded the house. When Ed was gone, I would drag a chair to the middle of the room and curl my legs under me. Stepping on them made a sickening crunch, so I'd wait for Ed to come home to take care of the roach population! Since we lived in a Filipino area, late in the evenings we could hear Filipinos singing and playing guitars, a pleasant way to go to sleep.

Leaving Peking February 28, 1941.

Chapter 5
Only too soon were those carefree days over

In the spring of 1941, school began with five Chinese teachers from Peking and about fifty students, who all met in the Masonic building. At first it seemed like a safe haven. A number of us decided that it was a good time to start a family since most of us had postponed this due to travel, study and uncertain conditions. It became a source of humor as all our pregnancies became apparent. At one party, one of the doctors stood up and said he had an announcement to make. He said, "My announcement is that my wife is not pregnant!"

Early in my pregnancy, we sent to Sears in the United States for a very extensive layette. Fortunately, it arrived before the Japanese, and I was able to share it with others in Camp. Sears also had a screened folding crib. We showed the picture to a clever Filipino carpenter who was able to duplicate it perfectly. So, planning for our baby, language school studies, and some social life kept us all occupied.

During the summer, Ed and Rolland were asked by Carl Eshbach, the pastor of Union Church, to go on a trip to visit his denomination's church missions among the Igorot people. Ed relates it as follows:

The Rev. Carl Eshbach was pastor of the Union Church of Baguio, a part of the mission effort of the United Brethren Church and a good friend to all of us in the Chinese language school. After a few months of study we were to enjoy a week's vacation. Carl invited Rolland Flory and me to accompany him on a trip to visit a few of the mission stations of the United Brethren Church north of Baguio. These missionary efforts were among the Igorot people of various tribes, all quite distinct in language and separated by customs. The trip was made in an

22

open-air bus over the winding mountain road not much more than a trail. We would have to wait at times for the road to be cleared of landslides. We stopped for the night at the local hotels, very simple in accommodations.

The Igorot people we met were the Bontoc, Ifugaos, and Ilocanos. We visited their churches in Bontoc, Kiangau and finally at Lubuagan. This is where I first met Leora and Ed Nagle. They had, at Lubuagan, a thriving church and a high school.

On our homeward trip with Carl we saw the Benaue rice terraces, one of the Seven Wonders of the World. We went further south by San Fernando on the coast where the Carl Widdoes lived and worked at the church there. It was a rewarding trip. After the war began, the Widdoes were brought to our camp and later were transferred to Los Banos Camp.

When the war began, the Nagles decided to stay in Kiangan, high in the mountains of northern Luzon. Eventually, Ed Nagle joined the American forces as a chaplain, and Leora hid with the Igorots from May until August of 1942, when the Japanese sent for her to surrender. She and two other American women missionaries eventually arrived at Camp Holmes.

Ed Nagle went south with the troops, later to be captured and imprisoned in Bilibid Prison in Manila. (This was the prison where our whole camp was moved to towards the end of the war.) In December of 1944, Ed Nagle was sent to Japan on an unmarked ship. Leora, in the Camp Holmes group, arrived in January of 1945 at Bilibid, missing her husband Ed by only a few weeks.

Because of impossible conditions, the unmarked ships were called Hell Ships. American planes or subs, not seeing any Red Cross markings, bombed the ships. Ed Nagle was rescued and taken to the city of Mogi on Kyushu Island. (It was the very city where we had stopped to refuel on our way to China.) There they had a prisoner-of-war hospital where the men were in desperate condition. Ed Nagle took dedicated care of them. His commanding officer later told Leora that Ed had worn himself out doing this. Sadly, he contracted dysentery and died of starvation.

This is only one of the terrible tragedies of those horrible years. The Japanese ignored any Geneva Convention rules of conduct in caring for prisoners of war, whether civilian or military. Leora did not learn of her husband Ed's cruel treatment and death until the end of the war, in August of 1945.

One of the happiest interludes during the first few months in the Philippines took place when the Bill Junkins, the Joe Smiths, the Don Zimmermans, the Jack Vinsons, and Ed and I went south to the San Fernando Beach for a week's vacation. Memories flood back:

(1) Ed and Bill took Jessie and I, their very pregnant wives, in an outrigger canoe in the China Sea, a pretty ridiculous sight.

(2) The men bought a huge fish early in the morning, as the Filipino fisherman pulled in his nets, lugging it back to the cottages and taking an hour to decide how to clean and prepare it. (Theologians always seem to get into lengthy discussions over everything.)

(3) Don Zimmerman told us stories at the campfire each evening and his ability to hold us all in suspense.

(4) Our reversion to child-like craziness as the men caught small crabs and put them underneath their caps on the dining room table. As the crabs moved so did the caps!

Only too soon were those carefree days over and we returned to Baguio and our language study. Several months later, the Japanese landed at that very same beach along with several other areas on Lingayen Gulf with forty-three thousand troops from eighty-five transports, some of whom came up to Baguio to make us "Guests of the Japanese Emperor!" Others went down to Bataan and headed on into that fearful conflict of war crimes and savagery.

Chapter 6
Life changed from that moment.

As the months passed, it became evident that relations between Japan and the United States were worsening. In mid-summer of 1941, we were told by city officials to begin black-out practices. Henry Luce, Francis Sayre (the high commissioner to the Philippines) and John Hayes (the head of our school) had been raised together as "Mish kids" in China. Dr. Hayes invited them to come to our Chinese language school.

Once there, we asked them about the political situation. There was a growing concern among us as to whether or not we should stay in the Philippines. Sayre replied that there might be attacks on Manila, but felt that since Baguio was a rather remote town it would be safe.

Ironically, the day that Pearl Harbor was bombed, Baguio was bombed as well.

In late November, our landlady, who lived next door, came over extremely distraught and in tears. Her husband was a high ranking officer in the Filipino Army, and he had called her that morning and told her to send their young ten-year-old son down to Manila. He told her that the boy would be safer in Manila because of rumors of war. She asked me what she should do. I suggested that since her husband probably had access to confidential information that we knew nothing about, it was probably best to follow his advice. Just a few short days later, Pearl Harbor was attacked, along with Baguio. I often wonder how surprised some people in Washington really were. After all, black outs and rumors had been around all summer.

The following is from Ed's diary of the first stressful and unbelievable days of the war:

Language study continued even after Sayre had told us that war with Japan may be imminent, but that we were not to worry, that the Philippines could be defended.

Life went on rather normally until December 8, 1941, which in Hawaii was the seventh. We went to school after hearing by radio of the bombing of Pearl Harbor and the declaration of war by President Roosevelt. During the morning of that day planes were heard and then, unbelieving, we learned they were Japanese planes, confirmed by the fact of the bombing of Camp John Hay, the U.S. base in Baguio. Needless to say that was the last day of school.

Our lives had taken another unexpected turn. There were meetings and discussions as to what we were going to do. The outcome of our best thoughts was that we would stay where we were and do what we could for each other and the community.

One of our first ideas was to set up an air raid warning system for the town. Accordingly we decided to use the highest peak, Santo Tomas. Several of us at a time were to hike up to the top and, with binoculars, watch for approaching Japanese planes. Then we were to phone to our air raid center, the local fire station, which would set off the fire sirens. I took my turn, having to leave Helen alone for some days.

Others worked on removing the beautiful stained glass windows from Union Church. We all tried to dig crude shelters and store food. The military had left in great confusion from Camp John Hay to join other American forces, going to Bataan, we were later to learn.

We had not long to wait. Toward the end of December, just three weeks after the start of the war, the Japanese fleet was seen in Lingayen Gulf. They could be observed from a certain lookout in Baguio. Landings were made with little opposition and the Japanese troops were on their way up the mountains to Baguio. At this point many of the civilians decided to band together at Brent School. The rape of Nanking was in everyone's mind and we felt we were safer to be together when the turnover occurred. We did not want to be in our houses and picked up individually for internment. So we were at the Episcopalian Brent Boarding School when the Japanese Army arrived in Baguio. In the middle of the night they entered the school grounds and gave orders for all of us to assemble outside. We never were permitted to go back into the buildings where we had left our few possessions, gathered quickly from our homes. The commanding Japanese officer told us that we were now "guests of the Japanese Imperial Army" and that we were to obey their orders. We were told to occupy only certain buildings. Guards were posted at the doors.

In this way we began a new life as internees, which would stretch out over three years. We were left at Brent for a few days with little water and food. Then we were ordered to march to Camp John Hay, the former American Army camp. We could take only what we could carry. The area of the camp where we were taken consisted of barracks that were surrounded by a chain link fence. Women were in one section, men in another and Chinese people in another. Japan was still at war in China but the Chinese were kept interned for only a few weeks.

The first morning of the war we were all shocked, in total disbelief that the attack had finally come. There were a few things that we still needed for the baby, who was due in January, so I decided to make a quick trip to downtown Baguio. Also, I was curious to see how the local Japanese were reacting. They had several shops on the main street, and as I walked down the street and made some purchases, including several lipsticks, I remember thinking this frivolous thought, "I can't be caught in a war without lipstick!"

When the Japanese arrived, I had my lipstick alright, but we quickly found out we could do without many of the things we had always thought of as absolute necessities. Lipstick was certainly the least of our worries as the war continued. But others thought of lipstick also –much to the relief of my guilty conscience for being so frivolous. After months of internment, one of the scientists in camp bought all of the boxes of Crayola that camp into the camp store to make his own brand of lipstick. I was really ticked at that, for I had hoped to get some of those crayons for the art classes I was teaching in the Camp Holmes School.

I don't remember seeing any Japanese merchants on my last shopping spree. Everything downtown was unnaturally quiet. Then I heard planes high overhead and thought, "How great! Our Air Force is protecting us!" At that very moment, I heard the heavy thud of bombs dropping, a terrifying sound. They hit Camp John Hay. One tragedy of that bombing was that an officer's wife was severely injured as she threw her body over that of her small son. As a result, she lost her leg, but the child was only slightly injured.

As Ed said, "Life changed from that moment, forever." Over the next three years we learned lessons in life of living, dying, giving, and receiving that would never be forgotten. While we never would have chosen internment, and the days of uncertainty, horror, boredom and rumors of the return of the Americans that went along with it, we still cherish the friends and memories of those tragic, sometime comical and crazy days when several cultures, prisoners and guards alike tried to maintain sanity and life on a lonely mountain top overlooking lovely Trinidad Valley.

Chapter 7
Chaos reigned...

After the bombing, but before our interment, life in Baguio and all over the islands changed drastically. Japanese planes flew over the city regularly. The fire sirens wailed warnings of incoming planes, and people scurried for any source of shelter. Floods of people from Manila and other lowland towns arrived daily, trying to avoid facing war in a large city. Others frantically packed up their belongings and rushed down to Manila thinking it would be better defended. Filipinos were issued rifles with which to fight.

After the first bombing, Ed went to the Post Office and sent a cable to Elgin, our church headquarters, to let them know we were all safe. As he emerged from the Post Office, a Japanese plane flew overhead. The Filipinos, having all been armed, began to fire at the plane, an impossible target. There was also random gunfire up and down the street as nerves were shattered and hysteria took over. Ed dove for a ditch, wondering if he would have to revise the cable he had just sent.

Chaos reigned. Some of the leading city officials left, including the American Chief of Police. Baguio had just purchased a new fire engine and, since it was new, they drove it into the mountains to prevent it from being damaged. Taxis with trees tied to their radiator caps as camouflage tore up and down the streets. The Red Cross representative left for Manila with all the funds. Food stores closed one by one as they ran out of supplies.

Radio news broadcasts from Manila occasionally told us that all was well and to stay tuned. Incessant music played. One tune played more than others was "Roll out the Barrel"--maybe they thought a bottle of beer might calm our nerves. Rumors were rife.

One day all the Americans were ordered to meet at a hotel to review our situation. I was visiting Jo Flory at the time in their apartment, and she and I decided to cut across Burnham Park opposite from the hotel. Along the way, we noticed some large sewer pipes had been placed at intervals all over the grass. We were half way across when Filipino soldiers started to yell at us to get off the area. Since we were half way there, we kept running until we reached the sidewalk. A soldier told us Japanese planes were due to land there any moment, hence the sewer pipes to prevent that from happening. Just another wild rumor. Finally, out of breath, we reached the hotel, but no conclusion could be reached, so we all went home again.

Christmas was nearing but little planning was done, as war was on our minds rather than "Peace and goodwill toward men." Just before Christmas, the Japanese landing at Lingayen Gulf occurred and most of us decided to gather at Brent School for our surrender. Officials from the city went down Naguilian Road with white flags, surrendering to the Japanese and declaring Baguio an open city. Reconnaissance planes were constantly flying low over Brent School. Gasoline tanks had been stored nearby and there was great concern that they might be hit.

Once, as I was walking from an air raid shelter up the hill to the dormitory, a small plane came zooming over only a few feet from the ground. I made a dive for a near-by shallow garbage pit and looked up at the plane. It was swooping so low I made eye contact with the pilot. A strange sinking feeling overtook me as I saw my first invader and knew that freedom for us would soon end.

Christmas day came and went. During a simple dinner prepared by a hastily gathered kitchen crew, there were three air raid alarms. We had to leave our dinner and go to a primitive shelter. By the third time I had tired of the whole business, and took my plate with me.

At midnight on December 27, 1941, the Japanese arrived at Brent School. We were summoned to go outside where they took our watches and car keys, and searched diligently for concealed weapons--even running their fingers in one woman's cold cream jar. Then we were told to gather in front of a building, where they separated the men, women, and children into separate groups. You can

31

imagine the terror parents felt as this happened. We were surrounded by soldiers and machine guns.

An officer, with a sword at his side, climbed on top of a desk that had been moved outside. It was Major Mukaibo (a Japanese Methodist minister, belonging to the Japanese Intelligence and educated in the States for college and seminary) who grimly greeted us. He was unrelenting in his hateful orders. Only afterwards did we learn of his

Welcoming Speech!

being a minister. One rumor was that he went to a seminary in Philadelphia, our home town and the City of Brotherly Love. I often wondered how he had fared as a Japanese person in the United States. He certainly bore a grudge and evidenced a steely expression as he announced that we were guests of the Japanese Imperial Army. If anyone escaped, three would be summarily shot. We were a thoroughly frightened, subdued group as we entered the dorm. There was one room where several older women were placed. I was directed there as well, since I was pregnant. That night, I slept on a hard window seat overlooking a court yard of search lights, machine guns, and soldiers - an eerie sight.

The next day Dr. Mather, one of the missionaries, checked on me. He found that my ankles had swollen. Since I had been bothered by toxemia during my pregnancy and thought to be in some danger, he asked the Japanese if I could be sent to the hospital. A young Japanese medic came and checked. Finally, patting my hand, he gave permission for me to go.

Continually during internment there were small gestures such as that, which reached across hate and cultural differences, and renewed our faith and hope for a future not bound by hatred but universal human understanding of one another. Over fifty years later, there are exciting ideas of peace, but bitter hatred and prejudices still exist. Sometimes I feel the whole world is interned by our own inability to love. The whole of human kind is imprisoned, longing to be free. It is still a race of survival.

At the hospital, I was put in the same room with Dr. Mather's wife Edith, who was already in Notre Dame Hospital having just given birth to Sally Ann. Edith related to me that the Belgium head nurse, a Catholic sister, had told her that this was good for Americans and that we would eat dirt before our release. The Filipino nurses, also Catholic sisters, were, on the other hand, very good to us.

While on my first stay at Notre Dame Hospital, a scene took place with truly comical, international overtones. The Catholic sisters were so sympathetic, looking after us with loving care. This particular Belgium order of sisters wore headdresses with wide flaring wings of white on each side. One day the nurse came in and told one of the patients that she must be given the dreaded enema. She bustled about with the dilapidated bag and upon inserting the hose, realized that the contents were not going through. To make it flow with more force she resourcefully, if not precariously, climbed upon a high-legged stool to administer her duties.

Just at that moment, one of the Filipino doctors arrived with two high ranking Japanese officers on an inspection tour of the hospital. The doctor was visibly nervous as he explained to the officers why American women were there, indicating pregnancy by a bulging motion of his hands over his stomach. Upon seeing the Japanese officers, the sister, from her high perch, with headdress benevolently over all, resorted to using her rosary with one hand, held the bag with the other and murmured a fervent prayer.

During the startling turn of events, I looked over at the patient of the usually-privately-administered-procedure. At first I thought she was crying, but instead she was overcome with a bad case of the giggles. She tried to control them by covering her face with the sheet. Fortunately, it did not turn into an international incident, and the doctor ushered the officers out of the room as quickly as he could respectfully do so.

Chapter 8
"So the feared was happening."

The following account is from Ed's diary. Anything in brackets in the following record are my comments as I copy this in 1994. Ed's diary is only of the first few months, as it then seemed prudent to stop writing an account concerning our treatment. It begins with the Chinese Language School and our discussions concerning our course of action since the beginning of the war...

There was nothing definite presented from the Army authorities, even though a few of the men had been to the camp and sought their advice. We were told that the American defense line would be to the south, leaving Baguio on the outside. However, if a large group as large as ours traveled behind the intended line there would be extreme difficulty in finding accommodations either in Manila or any other place. Therefore, practically all were of the opinion that we should remain where we were, come what may, and continue our present duties whatever they happened to be. Pastor Eschbach jokingly expressed that if and when the Japanese came, we would go on working for them instead of the Americans!

Tuesday, December 23: We were awakened by a knock at the front door by our neighbor who brought news that the Japanese Army was nearing the city and that all Americans should go to the Pines Hotel. How quickly we packed two suitcases, one for each of us. The dawn was breaking; it was 6:30 A.M.

So the feared was happening. It was not hard to believe because of the news the last few days made us rather expect it. It seemed to be a good idea for Americans to be in one place.

On the way we stopped at the Flory's place. Here, Helen waited while I went back home for my passport which I had forgotten in the rush. Then the four of us started out. We had just about reached the corner when the air-raid signal sounded. The nearest shelter happened to be the United Evangelical Church. We reached it about the time the planes flew over. Nothing happened and the all clear was given and we went our way.

We thought we would save some time if we cut across the park. Haste was our only idea. We soon regretted this move because planes were coming and here we were out in the open without any kind of shelter nearby. We went faster than ever, reached the edge of the park and confronted native soldiers, who urged us to hurry to the buildings on the opposite side. More troops were pouring out of the buses which were driving up all around us. What could all the hurry mean? Were the Japanese actually in sight and were these men getting ready for a fight? Then it occurred to me that these men were headed for the place of fighting and were taking shelter from possible bombings.

We finally reached our destination. The Pines Hotel was the most fashionable in town and here we were all over the lobby in assorted dress and appearance. Coffee and tea were served which was very refreshing as we waited and wondered what was going to happen. It gradually came to our attention that the danger was not as near as at first believed. After ascertaining the truth, the crowd began to disperse. We were told that it would be better for us to return to our homes and await further developments.

A system for keeping the scattered families informed as to the decisions of the civilian committee was organized. We made our way home, not as hurriedly or eventfully as our earlier flight. These activities had only taken part of the morning; other events were yet to happen.

Not long after we had reached our home, the third bombing of Baguio occurred. There was a lone plane circling around. This was heard plainly as Helen and I took refuge in a room we thought the safest in the house. There was only one set of windows and these were sheltered fairly well by the next door house. For this reason we had no view but this did not keep us from knowing the movements of the plane.

Suddenly we heard the sickening sound of the plane going into a dive. It is a dreadful noise, especially since we could not see where the plane was. We could only hear the unmistakable zoom and hope it did not come from directly overhead. Then we heard the explosion, louder than we had ever heard. What had been hit we could not tell. Later we learned that the power plant had been the probable target but that was untouched while some residences had been damaged. If there were casualties, we do not know.

While I was on duty at the school, word came that there would be a meeting of representative civilians at Brent School at twelve o'clock noon. No time could be lost so I started immediately to the district assigned to me. That had been the plan worked out that same morning. A few from our section attended the meeting, but I stayed behind to await the news. After the informants returned, we heard that Brent School was being made the place where all Americans could concentrate, if they desired. It was felt by the committee that the group should stay together in order to be ready for any eventuality. Once again we got ready to move. This time we were not hurried, as we needed to take time to plan and move more supplies because we did not know how long we would be away.

Brent School was located three or four miles from our place. Because there was no longer any sure way of transportation, it was decided the women folks should start walking while the men got the baggage together and get it transported in any way possible.

In these plans we were working with the Cunninghams and Florys. The ladies and little Larry started off, accompanied by Dr. Cunningham. He soon returned with the welcome news that Dr. Nance, Helen's personal physician, volunteered to drive them in his car. That was a great kindness in time of need. We finally found a car, the owner of which said he would be glad to help move our luggage. We piled in everything we could, leaving room for Dr. Cunningham who went to help the driver.

Rolland and I started to follow on foot. It was necessary to travel through the center of town. So we started up the familiar main street, Session Road, now looking strange because of the boarded up shops and the lack of people and cars. While strolling leisurely along, all of a sudden we heard the crack of rifle shots in front of us. We quickly jumped into the doorway of a shop. With an occasional glimpse from our hiding place we noticed a commotion on the street ahead. During a lull, we emerged and started on our way again but instead of following a direct route we turned into a side street moving a little faster.

Along the way we asked a bystander what the trouble was. The answer came, "Some Japanese civilians escaped from Camp John Hay and the guards are trying to get them." A little further on, we asked another young man who was cocking his rifle, "What are you shooting at?" "I don't know!" he answered unexpectedly.

By night fall, quite a number of Americans were "settled" in Brent School. Of course there was some doubling up necessary, but on the whole everyone was fairly comfortable. We and the Joseph Smiths shared a room.

Brent School is a private prep school named after Bishop Brent, an Episcopalian. The institution is now only partly under the mission board of that church. It is very popular among young people all over the Islands. Most of the students were able to reach their parents when the war first started but about fifteen boys and girls were unable to get away. This place was thought suitable for all of us because of the accommodations. There are several dormitories besides different school buildings, all in a spacious beautiful campus.

December 24, 25, 26: We hardly knew it was Christmas time. Because we did not do our Christmas shopping early, we missed the usual kind of celebration. Most others were in the same situation, however, and with other things to occupy our minds, the days quickly passed. Christmas was just like the day preceding and the day following.

The matters of chief concern were the transportation of supplies from homes and the digging of air raid shelter. On the other hand, rather than these hard duties, the chief objects of interest were the bits of news and rumors which drifted in our midst at Brent.

Various committees were responsible for the well-being of all. Some of the rumors came into reality. We had been hearing of the large fleet which had steamed in Lingayan Gulf. Our men who were "spotting" from Santo Tomas Mountain counted 90 to 110 ships. We had heard of the successful landing and of troop's advance through the lowlands. This day, there could be no doubt that Baguio was one of their objectives. Since the American Army had abandoned the city and left it unprotected it was thought by the civilians that an effort should be made to avoid needless destruction. Accordingly a committee was formed.

(The ex-mayor of Baguio and engineer, a trusted and beloved man, Mr. Halsema was put in charge after the officer, Horan, in charge of troops at Camp John Hay, abandoned the city. He informed Halsema as he was leaving, that he, Halsema, would be in charge of the city. The troops had left previously in utter confusion and Horan set off to find them. Horan made one brilliant move by putting Mr. Halsema in charge as he was respected by Anglos and Filipinos alike. It was at this time that Police Chief Keith, retired Colonel Pedro Dulay, and the son of a prominent Japanese business man, Henry Hayakawa, met at the edge of town and negotiated with the victorious Japanese to declare Baguio an "open city."

We were together eating in the dining room when Mr. Halsema made the announcement that they had contacted the advanced guard through a local Japanese interpreter and had arranged for the surrender of the city. They were also told of an attack plan. That afternoon the small group of forty-two men came into Baguio. They were followed by other units. This general news we could survey from our high point outside the center of town. Through the trees we could catch glimpses of the increased traffic on the road leading into town, which could mean only one thing. Besides, at various times we could hear the welcoming shouts and cheers of the local Japanese arising from the direction of the Japanese school, a place of concentration for them. In the twilight and following nightfall, the flashes of automobile headlights sparkled over the foliage as the Army kept moving into Baguio. Not knowing when we would be "called upon," we decided to go to bed. We posted our own lookout and retired to get what rest we could.

We were not kept in suspense very long. First, a small group came and requested all the cars that belonged to us. By this time there were quite a few parked on the grounds. The owners turned over their keys and resignedly watched the first act of confiscation; some never saw their cars again. Others saw them more or less frequently at the entrance of our camp, being enjoyed by Japanese officers.

The second visit came shortly after midnight. Our own men had prepared themselves for whatever might happen. As it turned out the occupants of each building were lined up outside and searched. (While we were being searched, Japanese soldiers searched our rooms. One thing we found missing when we returned was a gold pocket watch which had belonged to Ed's father. It was the only thing Ed had been given after his death, so though it was a small loss compared to others, there was a sad sense of what probably lay ahead of us.)

We were then ordered to march to the point on the campus where the main buildings were located. At the appointed place we met other groups who had been lodged in their quarters. When we left our temporary rooms we didn't realize how hard it was going to be to get back and gather a few personal belongings. So we had come with only the clothes we were wearing. It was quite a subdued group who listened to the few words and commands uttered by a Japanese officer. The general object was to collect all weapons we might have and to tell us we were responsible for each other, that if anyone made a false move all would suffer. (He said if one escaped 10 men would be shot.)

The final order was for all of us to spend the rest of the night in the boys' dormitory, women and men occupying opposite ends of the building. Due to crowding, the constant arrival of other Americans, and thoughts of our fate, little sleep was had during the few remaining hours until daylight.

The new day brought many things, one a blessing in disguise for us personally. The excitement, added to the condition of Helen's pregnancy, was not proving too good for her physical well-being. The doctors decided to send her to the hospital. Of course, permission would be a big obstacle; however, we were greatly relieved and encouraged when permission was granted and the order carried out. Naturally, I felt sad and lonely when the ambulance carried Helen away, but this meant she was to be spared much inconvenience and the upset conditions of the next few days.

Ed's diary of the first days of the war and internment ends here. When we arrived in San Francisco in March 1945, the FBI met the passengers and confiscated all diaries to check them for security reasons because of the war. Later on they returned them. This happened to Natalie Crouter's diary of 4,000 pages, the diary from which the book Forbidden Diary was later written, a very detailed story of our internment. It was misplaced for ten years, and finally surfaced in a storehouse in Kansas.

Chapter 9
Strangers were next to strangers...

Since I had missed the trip from Brent School to the Camp John Hay barracks, I was curious as to what life would be like there. Cases of dysentery were brought in daily from our internment camp, and the stories told by these patients were extremely grim. There was a water and food shortage, crowded conditions and severe, cruel orders by our guards. When I returned, friends filled me in on their experiences during the intervening days.

One story, edged with irony and humor, was of a young mother. While still at Brent School, she had somehow managed, in the chaos of three hundred people crowded into a dorm meant for sixty students, to wash diapers for her young son. Of course, there were no clotheslines. People were forbidden to leave the building, so she asked a guard at the door if she could hang the diapers outside on a near-by bush. The guard told her "No!" This was by gestures to one another. She persisted. Finally, the young guard, in desperation at this forward woman, not patterned after submissive Japanese women, looked around cautiously, handed her his rifle, and hung the diapers on the bush himself!

When the internees were marched two miles from Brent School to Camp John Hay, exhausted, hungry, and carrying heavy luggage, the Japanese had expected the Filipinos to line the streets to watch the deep humiliation of the Americans. To their credit, not a single Filipino stood and watched. They stayed indoors for that time. Throughout the entire war, our harsh treatment was tempered by loyal and brave Filipinos who sent in messages and food whenever they could. When they passed by on the road at Camp Holmes, some Igorots even whistled "God Bless America," even leaving gardenias by the roadside from time to time for our garbage crew to pick up on their way to the dump. The garbage crew would jauntily return pushing a heavy, dirty old cart wearing gardenias in their hat bands.

When Allied Forces returned to reclaim their lost territories, the Filipinos were the only organized native guerrilla group to welcome back their former conquerors. They do not deserve the fate of unbelievable poverty and political unrest that they are experiencing today.

When the internees were first taken to Camp John Hay they were all put in one barrack: men, women, and children. Strangers lived alongside strangers, undressing and sleeping, existing each day in view of five hundred

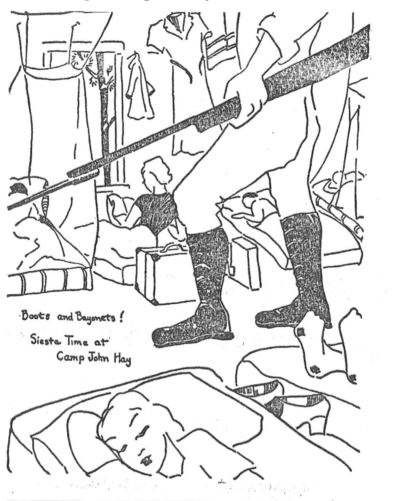

Boots and Bayonets!

Siesta Time at Camp John Hay

The Garbage Crew ...

fellow internees. Perhaps this is when one of our camp
mottoes originated, "If you want privacy, close your eyes."

Everyone slept on the floor with or without mattresses.
Some people brought in their mosquito nets, which hung
over their beds to protect them while sleeping. One woman
strung hers up on wires and pinned it around the edges of
the mattress. She tucked her little boy in and joined him
in bed. That night, as the man next to her got up to go to
the bathroom, her mosquito net was suddenly ripped down
around her. Apparently she had pinned one corner of the
net to the man's pajama leg!

Each night, Japanese guards, carrying rifles, tramped
noisily through the barracks keeping close watch over all
their "guests." Occasionally, they would bang the butts of

their rifles on the floor to emphasize some order, which only added to the unrest of hungry children and adults trying to lose themselves in sleep. To make matters worse, there were times when there was not any water because of the failure of the pumping system. Drinking water had to be brought in by truck, and rationed at two cups a day. Food was also extremely scarce and rationed as well. It was at this time that dysentery began to take its hold, and some people who became severely ill were permitted to go to Notre Dame Hospital.

Chapter 10
Only a few months...

By the first few weeks of 1942, we had finally faced the reality that it would probably be at least "a few months" before the American forces returned. Rumors circulated constantly about a possible early return. Unfortunately, they were only rumors—our confinement was to last thirty-seven months. Early on we tried to create a semblance of order and routine. Still murmuring to ourselves, "only a few months," we carried on our daily existence.

Some of the men decided that they were not going to shave until the Americans returned. That was as good an excuse as any. Even in the best of conditions, men fuss about shaving, but with crowded bathrooms, no mirrors, and shortages of soap and water, this was the perfect time to declare independence from one more daily chore. The beards that emerged were fearsome to behold. Since our men were larger than the average Japanese and presented a hairy abundance unfamiliar to the Japanese male, it must have been intimidating to guard these wild-appearing enemies.

Lloyd Cunningham grew a particularly luxuriant beard, of which Ellen was less than enthusiastic. He was just about to shave it off due to her needling when one of the British ladies told him he looked like the former king, and the beard remained. Ed grew a beard but after awhile only sported a moustache. (When we returned home, he kept this camp souvenir. As part of his duties as a returned missionary, he was obliged to speak in various churches. One church wrote to the mission board and reported that Ed was wearing a moustache saying it looked "too military." They wanted him to shave it off because the Church of the Brethren was one of the original peace churches. So his moustache disappeared forever. The Lord giveth and the Church taketh away...)

47

After the first few days of being crowded into one barrack regardless of sex, the Japanese decided to move the men next door, which made life less embarrassing in regards to dressing and bathroom use. At first, the use of the bathroom was restricted to one hour for the men and the next hour for the women. The barracks' bathroom consisted of a long row of toilets, without stalls, but with a partition in front of them, and a row of wash basins in the center of the room. There were no mirrors--not exactly a Kohler-appointed decor.

After the men left, some supplies came in of varied sorts. Our women's committee triumphantly put curtains between each "john" for a bit more privacy. While the men were still in residence, we had to station a "distributor of toilet paper" at the entrance to the bathroom. This was a precious commodity and had to be doled out fairly, and we were allowed two pieces per trip. A good male friend whose identity will go unknown, one day slipped me a third piece with a wicked wink. How's that for true friendship?

The camp committee, hastily formed with Japanese permission, also helped decide the distribution of food, of which there was very little. One lunch consisted only of the boiled water in which hot dogs had been cooked for a former meal. Because the committee was concerned about the health of small children and pregnant women, we were allowed an extra snack each day. When it was time for said snack, an older man would yell at the top of his voice, "Small children and expectant mothers, line up!"

I was embarrassed to be the recipient of special favors, but concern about the safety of our baby overpowered my embarrassment. It was hard on the children in their teens, who did not receive any extras, because that is a time of real growth. One morning, I saw one of these kids in the bathroom squeezing an inch of toothpaste into his mouth. He said that it was his daily ration of candy. I'm sure his mother wondered about the quick disappearance of toothpaste, which for all of us soon became a luxury of the past. It was an embarrassment to make such public ablutions for those with dentures and other personal rituals of daily care. One proud elderly woman always went early to the bathroom to brush her wig in some privacy, as at that time wigs were not exactly a fashion statement.

The elderly people in our camp were amazing in their attitude toward internment. They were the ones who had the most to lose as we younger folks still hopefully had our lives before us. During all the three years, they stoically bore the indignities of camp life, painfully aware that their fortunes could never be recovered.

Now that I am elderly myself, and familiar with the aches and pains of old age, I am filled with more admiration and respect for them than ever before. For the most part, they worked with good humor alongside the rest of us. Perhaps it was because many of them had come to the Islands twenty, thirty or forty years before and had endured the hardships of setting up homes, businesses, schools, and government services when the Spanish withdrew. These people, along with the Filipinos, had built a prosperous life for most of the citizens of the Philippine Islands. Even though all of that was now gone, their humor and grace remained.

When the men moved to the barracks next door, more room for daily existence was welcomed, but it was still crowded. One night a youngster near my mattress went to the bathroom. When he returned, he was confused at the long row of mattresses in a dark barrack, and he crawled in bed with me. I had to gently lead the sleepy little fellow to the correct mama and mattress.

I suppose it seemed perfectly natural to have the mattresses on the floor to our "hosts," but for us it was just one more discomfort, especially for those of us who were pregnant. To have to lurch, scramble and pull oneself up each morning was not a pretty sight.

One day, the Japanese announced that we were to hand over all of our money, and it was rumored that they were going to take our jewelry as well. I immediately went to the bathroom to conceal my engagement ring with a hairpin in my long hair. Resentment ran high that day as we had to meekly line up and part with what little money we had. There seemed to be no end to the constant harassment and humiliation heaped upon us.

A Swedish consul's wife had been mistakenly interned with us. Diplomatic personnel were not to be interned according to international law, and her husband in Manila had arranged her release. As she prepared to leave, after a few days of incarceration, she said, "Now, I'm going home and have myself a nervous breakdown!" Sadly, the rest of us were not given that choice, and we resignedly settled down to face our most pressing problem, survival.

The people of the Baguio community played a key role in this. After our internment, these same people continued in their role of go-betweens for the internees and the Japanese. "They" were the counselors, who solved the problems faced by the five hundred people of varying cultures, beliefs and value systems thrown together unexpectedly. It was a task even Solomon would have hesitated to assume, and yet these people, often at great risk to themselves, performed in a manner that earned them the titles of heroes and heroines. I hesitate to name them individually for fear of omitting someone, but those of us who experienced their care and wisdom will be forever grateful. We are here because of them. As I continue to relate our story, some of these people will be mentioned but by no means will this be the total.

According to the Japanese, this was to be a hundred years war, and there was no need for a school because the kids would be old men and women before they ever could think of being released.

As the middle of January 1942 approached, Ed and I knew that the inevitable was fast approaching, and that our greatly anticipated first born would soon arrive to face life in an internment camp. Of course this was not our hope. We all knew that the Americans would return soon. Rumors fed this optimistic feeling in the early days of the war. The Japanese idea of a century long war and our idea of a quick release were, in a way, a subtle comedy as we tried to exist in our roles of guard and guarded.

Perhaps the word comedy is a strange one to use. However, there were many times when a tension-filled situation occurred, and after it was momentarily or finally resolved, we were able to have a good laugh. For one instance, the story of the guard and mother in pantomime working out the problem of who was going to hang the diapers on the bush. The Japanese constantly amazed us with their attitudes toward things to which we felt quite the opposite way, like the day when a Japanese flag was carelessly draped over the fence in front of the woman's barracks, and a Japanese soldier nonchalantly used it as a handkerchief.

With approximately sixty children of all ages in the women's barracks, pandemonium reigned a great deal of the time. In response, classes were organized by a few teachers from Brent and some missionaries. After a week of this, the Japanese informed us of our lengthy stay and the fact that education was, therefore, unnecessary. Classes were officially disbanded, but quietly resumed as much for the sake of the adults' sanity, as the educational value for the children. The classes were usually held on someone's mattress, as the students and teacher sat in informal array, learning their ABC's.

At the same time, we were learning the ABC's of communal living. At times, tensions between internees ran high. One of the pregnant women had kept a few crackers for herself after everyone had given up their small supply of food to the common kitchen. She was caught munching on these. It only took three weeks of intense hunger for another woman to grab her by the hair and loudly denounce her act.

A friend, a well-educated and cultured woman, later told us that if at that time she had had a chance to steal food she would have done so. It doesn't take long for our survival instincts to overpower the veneer of culture and learning. Today, I believe we see this in relation to the horrors of crime and hopelessness in our own beloved country; without hope and vision, a people perish.

Fortunately for us, reason prevailed and the beginning of an orderly system of living and caring in camp evolved, slowly but surely.

Chapter 11
We were a small microcosm of life...

As the middle of January, 1942 approached. Ed and I knew that the inevitable was fast approaching, and that our greatly anticipated first born would soon arrive to face life in an internment camp. On the evening of the 17th of January, I began labor pains. I told Bessie Crim, our mission nurse, and she suggested that we go to the restroom as that was the only place lit at that time of night. After counting contractions, she suggested that I wait until morning as I might have a better chance of being taken to our local hospital.

At that moment, a Japanese guard appeared at the door. He was extremely agitated and reported that a Chinese woman in the Chinese barracks was about to deliver. Bessie, never one not to seize the moment, told him that I was also in labor and that he should get the supply truck, called the Black Maria, ready to go into town.

Bessie received permission to go to the men's barracks to get Dr. Nance, but she had no idea where Dr. Nance slept, so in the darkness she stumbled down row after row of hard-to-recognize bearded men. After being cursed roundly by more than just a few men, she finally found him. They then awakened Ed, but Dr. Nance told him it would not be feasible for him to go with us, and, besides, he would be in the way. Ed was able to come to the gate to say good-bye as we scrambled into the truck: Dr. Nance, Bessie, the Chinese lady, and me.

The Chinese lady was much nearer childbirth and half laid on what remaining lap I had. We stopped at the Baguio Hospital first to drop her off, and then proceeded on to Notre Dame Hospital. As we went up the steps, Dr. Nance said to me, "Honey, I want you to take a good long time at this, as I want to get three square meals from this trip." I told him I'd do my best if he didn't send me to delivery at meal time. Unfortunately, for me, he got his wish as I was in labor for 27 more hours before Carol Louise was finally delivered on the 19th of January, 1942.

Later that month, another mother went into labor. She had had another doctor, but the Japanese refused to allow them to go to the hospital. That was the first baby who was actually delivered in Camp. Later, that doctor came to the hospital, burst into my room, and informed me that it was my fault that they were not permitted to come to the hospital because Dr. Nance had been gone so long because of my lengthy delivery. I was shocked, but realized that tensions were high at this time. Neither Dr. Nance nor I had any control over the situation. Dr. Nance left as soon as the truck arrived, the day Carol was born.

These two doctors had a certain animosity between them. Later, when political parties emerged, their names were even attached to the two political parties for awhile. We were certainly a small microcosm of life in the world we had known. Americans cannot live without politics and committee meetings. It might be nice to try. Certainly reaching consensus is even more difficult in the midst of the hatred of war. We knew of atrocities of the war as it was waged with the battle cry of "East Asia for East Asians!" In no way do I want to explain away these acts. They were terrible then and terrible in retrospect. All wars are, but the miracle of our existence and survival resulted from Filipinos, our people, and some of the Japanese showing understanding of the plight in which we found ourselves.

Carol Louise weighed eight pounds and eight ounces and had bright, wonderful eyes and curly hair. She was a good baby right from the start. We were very fortunate that she was born at the beginning of our internment, while I was still healthy. As time passed, other women and babies had a much more difficult time. For some of these children, the poor nutrition they had before birth affected their future lives. Before he left the hospital, Dr. Nance, gave me strict orders to be a "good lunch counter" for her in the months to come, and I succeeded, later with some supplements to follow that order until she was almost a year old. "The food at the hospital!" is a cry we always seem to hear from anyone in the hospital even now, but that time of shortages and the fear of more to come, it was indeed sparse. I remember one meal was boiled pig skin with the bristles still on the skin.

The nurses followed usual hospital procedures of that time. Carol was brought to me only at nursing time. I tried to keep her with me, but they always came and took her back to the nursery, where she was all alone in a darkened nursery. I did not demur as everyone was under great pressures.

The Japanese constantly roamed the hallways—their constant presence a reminder that they were in power. At that time, the Filipino staff was protecting an injured American soldier who had lost contact with the Army. They passed him off as a civilian. On the floor below my room was an American dying of tuberculosis. He had a record player, which constantly played nostalgic records such as Home Sweet Home. As these sounds wafted up to my room, it was hard to keep a stiff upper lip.

I had decided early on in internment that under no circumstances would I cry. I kept to this promise to myself for the duration of the stay, and even after we returned home I found it difficult to give way to tears. The only time that I did so was when the U.S. Army Band stopped at Camp Bilibid and played the Star Spangled Banner, our beautiful flag flying freely above us.

During the time that I was in the hospital, the Japanese military police, similar to the dreaded Gestapo, began questioning the missionaries. They suspected the Chinese Language School students of being spies for the Chinese government. When we first arrived in Baguio, Ed and Rolland Flory were asked to teach English to a local Chinese group, which the Japanese later accused of having ties to mainland China. Rolland, being the son of former China missionaries, already had some knowledge of the Chinese language and did not have to study the language as intensely as Ed was obliged to do. It actually took hours of classes and home study every day, so Ed declined to help with this volunteer work.

When the Japanese took the missionaries in for questioning, they were particularly hard on those who had been teaching English to the Chinese community. Rufus Gray died under their severe water cure tortures. Rolland Flory and Herb Lattigs survived the same treatment, but they have suffered continuous health problems as a result of that horrifying experience.

Each day they took several men into town for questioning. The day that they brought Ed into town for this, Wally Moore, president of the local bank, was driving the camp truck. He stopped at the hospital for some supplies, and told Ed that when the truck stopped there, not to ask permission but to just dash into the hospital in order to see our new baby. It was risky as it could have startled the Japanese guards into action, but Wally explained the situation to the guards as Ed made his fast exit. Thus, before Carol and I returned to camp, Ed saw Carol and had a few moments with me. This was just another example of an internee helping a fellow internee. When Ed left, he went to be questioned. If his fate had been that of Rufus, at least he had gotten to see Carol.

After Carol was born, I was forced to stay in the hospital, and bed, for three weeks, as Dr. Nance was not permitted to come in to change orders or dismiss me. In the meantime, Bessie Crim, who had helped deliver Carol, was able to come see me on a trip to the hospital. It was a welcomed visit, camp news our chief topic of conversation.

On her return trip, the Japanese guards stopped at a restaurant. As they did not dare leave Bessie in the truck unguarded, they allowed her to join them. All the time she was there, the Filipino waitresses were surreptitiously slipping her hard boiled eggs. She had on her nurse's cape and hid the eggs in her uniform pockets until they were full. For the last egg she had no room, so she slipped it under her armpit. It was the only egg which was not hard boiled.

All of which reminds me of another experience involving eggs. Sometime after I returned to camp, one of our friends told me to meet her at dusk on the ditch side of the barracks. A Filipino friend had sent in some food. As we sat on the edge of the ditch, she handed me a supposedly hardboiled egg. As we opened them, we realized they were boloots (eggs which are not quite fully developed and considered a delicacy by the Filipinos). We were glad it was not quite dark and we could see our treat. As hungry as we were, we could not eat them. These are my two "eggstraordinary" stories.

During my lengthy, lonely stay in the hospital, Pastor Subido, the Filipino pastor of Union Church, visited me. He had risked going down to our house. The landlady had let him in, and he had collected a few valuables which he brought to me. It was a touching, loving visit by a brave person. Just coming to see me was a risk in itself. After the war, the Subido family came to Dayton, Ohio to attend United Seminary where we joyfully renewed our acquaintance.

Doctor Nance was finally permitted to come in, and I returned to camp. The new-born babies were assigned to the barrack's jail-room, which was a long, narrow, dark room with one small barred window. Not exactly the nursery of my dreams.

While I was in the hospital, the erratic, unpredictable Japanese had allowed all the missionaries to be released to their own homes. The next day the Chinese Language School missionaries were ordered back to camp. "There was no joy" in Camp John Hay, as the internees had to move back into smaller spaces to permit the return of these people. During that short time however, Ed was able to gather some baby clothing, diapers, and the collapsible canvas baby carriage that we had ordered from Sears, so when I returned, we had a safe, snug place for our baby. I had ordered a very generous baby wardrobe and supply of diapers from the States before the war, so it was a pleasure to have this abundance and be able to share with the two other babies as they arrived.

Another "luxury" I had was a cot, which Ed had looted while on the garbage crew. Each day Carl Eschbach and other missionaries, like beasts-of-burden, would shove and pull the garbage cart to a nearby dump at Camp John Hay. Carl became known as the "looting parson" because when they passed vacated U.S. officers homes on the return trip, he asked permission to go in and bring back essentials for camp life on the return trip. Once, Carl and the crew pushed and shoved a much-needed refrigerator onto the cart. Ed found a canvas cot and as they passed the back fence of camp, he threw it over so the guards in the guardhouse would not confiscate it. Then upon entering camp, he dashed around back and retrieved it. When I arrived back at the camp from the hospital that was my homecoming present. Even at that time, some were still on mattresses on the floor, so I was very fortunate. Ed always managed to come through for our family in one way or another.

Chapter 12
"Thanks for the roses along the road..."

At this point, I'm going to insert a diary of Ed's that I just found among our mementos of internment and had forgotten about in the passage of fifty years. It also contains a "calendar of events" of those crazy confused pre-internment days and the crazier existence we endured at the beginning of our internment. His record contains an immediacy about the situation that my account lacks due to the fact that mine stretches back to those long ago days in memory only.

I have tried not to refer to accounts written by other internees because I want to record only my own personal memories and feelings. I have referred to Renton Hinds' book, Spirits Unbroken, but only to ascertain certain dates. He kept a complete day-by-day record of the happening of our entire internment. I also phoned Betty Foley to verify names of places and important happenings.

The following are short notations of most days from December 22, 1941 until April 23, 1942. Words in brackets are mine.

Mon. Dec. 22 Meeting at school. Situation serious. Some advise heading South to get behind defense line. Majority opinion: all should stay. Bombing

Tues. Dec. 23 Routed out at 6:30 A.M. Go to Pines Hotel. Return. Bombing. In   evening go to Brent School. Room with the Joseph Smiths.

Wed. Dec. 24 Dig air raid shelters - little food.

Thurs. Dec.25 Transfer more goods from home. Air raids.

Fri. Dec. 26   Rumors.

Sat. Dec. 27   Japanese troops arrive in city. Hear shouting. American cars seized.

Sun. Dec. 28   1:00 AM. Called out. Searched. All to men's dorm. Helen had a bed. [not so - I had a window sill] I slept on a mattress with Lloyd and Rolly. No food. In afternoon a piece of Spam on half slice of bread. Helen permitted to go to hospital. Women and children put in dining hall.

Mon. Dec. 29   Went to Camp John Hay.

Tues. Dec. 30   K.P. duty.

Wed. Dec. 31   Day off. No water.

1942

Sun. Jan. 4   Group joined with others in storeroom. Jantzen spoke on Psalm 37. Men moved to next barracks. Lloyd, Rolly and I slept together. Very breezy.

Mon. Jan. 5   Worked. Helen came back from hospital to camp.

Tues. Jan. 6   No work. Get to see Helen twice a day when we go for meals.

Wed. Jan. 7   Inspection [?]

Thurs. Jan.   Eat in own dining room. All food cooked here [men's barracks]. I help carry over to women's side. Rain.

Fri. Jan. 9   Newcomers. Definite turn in the news.

Sat. Jan. 10   Money [collected by Japanese] all day job. Did not see Helen.

Sun. Jan. 11 Swedish consul arrives for his wife. He dampens news. In evening group on porch. Carl Eshbach leads in prayer.

Tues. Jan. 13 Daily routine. Roll call - 8:00 AM. Meal - 9 AM. Meal - 4 P.M. Lights out - 9:30 P.M. During women's roll call they instructed not to kiss husbands, walk arm in arm, sit too close.

Wed. Jan. 14 1:00 shooting. Airplanes cause quite a discussion. Tokyo reports sinking of "Lexington."

Sun. Jan. 18 Bessie woke me 3:30 AM. She also called Dr. Nance. I saw him and asked him to call W. Moore. I went to women's side. Waited at door for Bessie and Helen. Truck first picked up Chinese lady and Bessie then Helen, Dr. Allen and Dr. Nance. Went back to bed. In morning Wally Moore reports Chinese baby born five minutes after arrival at Baguio Hospital. Service at 11:00. Heard briefly from two sources. Helen Wells returned from hospital and said Helen was doing fine. Later Nance called about dysentery cases. He also said baby would probably come in the night. 6:00 P.M. vesper service. Don Zimmerman. Luke 6. Moffat.

Mon. Jan. 19 3:30 A.M. Carol born. About 7:30 A.M. while listening to Japanese lieutenant of Navy who was talking to informal group. Truck arrives with Nance and Bessie who brought news. Had heard previously while in tennis court [not to play tennis] waiting for roll call, because Nance had called on phone. Helen sent note.

Wed. Jan. 21 "Things which are not seen are eternal."

Fri. Jan. 23 Took ride. [This was for military police questioning. Ed did not state reason for "ride." Others stayed longer.]

Sat. Jan. 24 Interviewed. Back in 2 hours. Others sent. 2 kept. On way stopped and saw Helen and Carol.

Sun. Jan. 25 5 more. One did not return. Service in morning but no more to be permitted.

Mon. Jan. 26 Five more went and all returned. Bessie in to see Helen.

Tues. Jan. 27 Five went. One returned.

Wed. Jan. 28 18 went. All returned. One after spending the day. "Daily Light" - Don Z.

Fri. Jan 30 [This entry is about the time the Japanese released the missionaries for a few days. I was still in the hospital.]
Left about 2 P.M. to Baguio Hotel. [Lutheran seminary represented] 6:30 p.m. to hospital. Held Carol for the first time. Sister James brought me milk. Left about 7:30 P.M. on way. Made two trips carrying luggage to Lutheran apt. To Cunningham's for supper and to bed. All missionaries there except Rolland, Helen and Carol.

Sat. Jan 31 Up at 8 A.M. Told to meet at Baguio Hotel at nine. Went with baggage to our home. Had trouble opening door. Everything intact. All at hotel at 9:00 A.M. At 2:00 P.M. Start back to camp. Local Baguio missionaries set free. Brought in baby equipment.

Sun. Feb. 1 Informal service.

Mon. Feb. 2 Election day. Volleyball.

Tues. Feb. 3 Helen and Carol back.

Wed. Feb. 4 Committee sends letter to Red Cross in Manila requesting aid for us. 482 report of money on hand.

Thurs. Feb. 5 Above money ordered turned over.

Sun. Feb. 8 Took Carol on tennis court.

Mon. Feb. 9   Helped clean dining room. First day that men had lunch.

Tues. Feb. 10 Hospital underway. [This was building near barracks that interned doctors and nurses adapted into a primitive hospital as they no longer allowed use of Notre Dame Hospital.]

Thurs. Feb. 12 Fighting in streets of Singapore.

Sun. Feb. 15 Billy Junkin born.

Mon. Feb. 16 Peter Collier born. Sign - [Japanese placed on fence.] "Singapore has fallen!"

Feb. 15.   Received number tags. [These we had to wear to daily roll call.] Walk with family 6:30-7:00.

Wed. Feb. 18 High school started.

Sat. Feb. 21 Order: No School, meetings, etc.

Thurs. Feb. 26 Anniversary party on tennis court with Cunninghams and Jo F. Pomelo was refreshment. [A pomelo is a glorified grapefruit with sections like a navel orange.]

Sat. Mar. 21 Carabao. [I think this was day they shot a caribou for camp. Ed got the Japanese bullet which shot it.]

Fri. Apr. 3   Jimmy born. [Ed did not want to use last name of Flory as Rolland was still at military police jail.]

Sun. Apr. 5   Sunrise service. [Easter]

Fri. Apr. 10   Sign: Bataan fell finally with unconditional surrender. Apr. 9, 7 P.M. Now let us realize 'the Orient for the Oriental'

<u>Tues. Apr. 14</u> Rolland and Laddigs back.

<u>Thurs. Apr. 23</u> Moved to Camp John Hay. Total number in camp–477, missionaries-157, still left in Baguio-35
>
> Baguio bombings:
> Dec. 8
> Dec. 13
> Dec. 22
> Dec. 23

> Thanks for the roses along the road
> Thanks for the thorns among them
> Thanks for the ladder raised to heaven
> Thanks for the ever protected home.
>
> From Norwegian

(This poem Ed copied after we arrived home and placed it at the end of this dated diary account.)

Chapter 13
"You're just like us!"

February of 1942 brought disheartening news. Singapore had surrendered unconditionally. The defeat of this mighty bastion of the British Empire gave all of us a sense of defeat in our own lives. The wild rumors of our soon-release tapered off noticeably. To further exaggerate this feeling, one day the Japanese brought local Japanese school children to view the captured Americans assembled on the tennis court behind barbed wire. Don Zimmerman said, "It's surprising they did not bring peanuts to shove through the fence!"

I remember an incident concerning peanuts while we were in Peking. At that time all our mail was censored by the occupying Japanese. One of the single students had written to his mother. He put in a warning that our mail was censored and to be cautious what she wrote to him. He used the derogatory term, saying, "Little monkeys open the mail." On that letter a Japanese censor had written, "Remember, little monkeys can read!"

Speaking of monkeys and peanuts, the same student had this humorous experience. One day at language school he had received word from the post office that a package awaited him from home. A visit to the post office for Americans in itself meant a half day wait, red tape and frustration to obtain the package. Finally receiving the package, he opened it. His mom had sent him pounds of shelled peanuts, knowing peanuts were one of his favorite treats and thinking her beloved son was without. But, alas, it was wasted expense and effort as hot roasted peanuts were sold on almost every corner in Peking. Well, so much for monkeys, peanuts, cultural differences and insults.

Daily routines evolved as camp committees and internees organized and carried out the daily chores of keeping everyone clean, alive, and fed on food that was grossly inadequate. It was during this time that the leaders in camp hammered out policies to deal with the Japanese in charge of our camp. One extremely wise policy was that only certain committee members were to contact the Japanese when problems arose. Thus we avoided situations where individuals might complain directly to the enemy with perhaps disastrous results for all of us. One of the most important and capable people so designated, was Nellie McKim, an Anglican second generation missionary whose father had been the Anglican bishop in Tokyo. She was familiar with the subtle nuances of bargaining, as well as the language, customs, and taboos of the Japanese people. She was one of the true heroines, who we are all deeply indebted to.

Another person that I would like to mention is Ruth Eshbach, Carl's wife. She was forced to return to the United States before the war because one of her children was losing his eyesight. During those long years of war, she had the task of caring for their children, seeing Bob, their son, through eye surgery, and dealing with the disheartening news of his impending blindness. Even though she was not present in camp, she was spoken of and remembered often. Once, when some of the women became entangled in wild arguments due to petty politics and cliques, someone mentioned that if Ruth had been there, her presence and wisdom would have forestalled many of these ever present issues. As many countless women at home bore heavy burdens, so too did Ruth with a flair and courage all her own. After the war, she was often hostess to reunions of internees held in Dayton, and she endured all our chit-chat and reminiscence of Camp life endlessly, day after day with humor and grace.

Daily roll call was held on the tennis court for the men. Each day, as the men passed the women's barracks, the new mothers would stand on the steps of the barracks with soiled diapers in pails and the fathers would take them back to their barracks, wash and dry them, and bring them back the next day at roll call time. There has never been a diaper service like that one. Care and love certainly embodied that act.

With only daily sweeping, scrubbing, washing of clothes, standing in chow line, and helping with communal chores to fill our time, the days passed slowly, punctuated by moments of terror as rumors and or edgy, angry Japanese guards swept through our barracks.

One of the first rules that the Japanese issued was that men and women were to be separated, that "co-mingling" would only be allowed once a week on the tennis courts, and that there was to be no kissing. The rumor that circulated was that the Japanese were familiar with the sleazy movies Hollywood shipped abroad, and their idea of American morality was pretty low.

Some of the Japanese guards expressed surprise that we had any form of family life at all. After a few months, one guard who had been observing us said, "You're just like us!" If left alone without politics and propaganda influencing us the world over, we would all find this to be true.

There was a certain spot in the back of both of our barracks where we could unobtrusively linger and catch a glimpse of our beloveds each day, a small, but comforting reassurance. When anyone from either of the barracks noticed a husband or wife on the other side standing around, someone would inform the spouse that they were there. Sign language became popular.

This was true except for the wives who had been inadvertently separated from their husbands because of the war's fickleness or the wives of three men who had been detained by the military police. Finally, Rolland Flory and Herb Lattigs returned, but there was still no official word of Rufus Gray's whereabouts. Marian Gray sat by the fence nearest the guard house, every day hoping that this would be the day Rufus returned. It was excruciating to watch her lonely vigils. His return was never to be, as Rufus died due to the torture. Rumors were rampant of his demise, but kept from Marian until it could be confirmed.

Carl Eschbach and other local missionaries were still free in Baguio. He received word that Jimmy had been born to Josephine Flory. He somehow got word to Rolland and then, to let Jo know that Rolly knew of his new son, he sent Jo a can of Johnson Baby Powder with inconspicuous lettering, "From Rolland." What a sad way to experience a usually joyful event.

When I returned to Camp with Carol, they allowed Ed to come over and he walked proudly all though the barracks, showing off our newborn. For an hour on Sundays, internees were permitted on the tennis courts with white lines painted seven feet apart. Standing on these lines separating us, women on one side and men on the other, we tried to express feelings and exchange news. Since I had the baby carriage, I wheeled Carol to the tennis court, gave the carriage a shove across the seven foot space, and Ed would play with her for the short time allowed.

On the 26th of February, 1942, our fourth wedding anniversary, we invited Jo and Rolly Flory and Ellen and Lloyd Cunningham to share a pomelo in celebration. (A pomelo is similar to a grapefruit which peels like a navel orange.) Such elegance as we tossed the segments to the men across the seven feet separating us. A pomelo is fairly sour and slightly bitter, which maybe was indicative of our feelings at that time.

Chapter 14
If anything is constant, it is change.

If anything is constant, it is change. It was surprisingly so even during our days of internment. Even there, the human diorama continued in a seemingly boring and restrictive existence.

One evening Lucy Vinson and I were visiting together on the porch of the women's barracks when we heard some commotion in the guard house just beyond the front of our barracks. Several cars with highly-ranked officers had descended upon them. After much terrifying yelling, the officers finally left, and quiet descended on our isolated internment camp. The starry, velvety sky of northern Luzon covered the scene of our imprisonment, and Lucy and I crept back into our allotted places among sleeping forms of prisoners, many on mattresses still on the floor. Thus began another long night filled with anxiety, wondering, and fear of the unknown future.

Later, we found out that the officers had thrown a big party in Baguio. Fortunately for us, some local Japanese were invited. As the revelry continued along with the drinking, one of the local Japanese overheard some of the officers planning to come out to our camp for a "jolly little shootout." The real possibility of a tragedy was present. The aforementioned Japanese hurriedly phoned the highest commanding officer in Baguio and told him what was about to take place. The officer immediately called the guard house, telling them that under no condition were they to allow the drunken officers into our camp; hence the ruckus.

All throughout our internment there were incidents just like this, which reminded us of how tenuous life can be. For some, it deepened their spiritual beliefs and faith in God, and for others a certain cynicism developed. We were truly a microcosm of the outside world within the crowded bounds of that camp. Through selfishness and generosity, faith and doubting, kindness and cruelty, we learned, laughed, grieved and endured for over three years. There were deaths and births, marriages strengthened and weakened, friends made and friendships broken, political parties formed and changed, church groups came closer together in times of peril, forgetting differences in theology then sadly drifted apart as tensions lessened. Deeper appreciation of our differences culturally and racially developed.

A rich panoply of activities and happenings occurred within that confining barbed wire fence that still brings former internees together, a bond that transcends even our feelings for our own family members. Laughter and tears are shared when we reminisce about those times. I think of various reunions, large or intimate, laughter prevailing over tears. Recently, I talked with Betty Foley about this phenomenon, and she likened internment to child birth; you forget the pain and remember the joy.

As the terrible war waged and swirled around us, we felt terror and hunger. We heard horrendous news of what was happening to the Filipinos, our military men in captivity, and those in hiding. Depressing thoughts filled our heads of what might happen during the fighting at the turnover, where as many people had died at Hiroshima and a whole city was destroyed beyond imagination. (Thankfully, when it actually occurred, we had been moved to Manila.) Yet the memories of daily problem solving, the deepening of friendships, the realization of how talented and resourceful the people with whom we were interned were, made those days of loss and fear less so. We settled into the routine of living in abnormal circumstances, but with a striving to survive with some cockiness and flair. Perhaps as Americans whose ancestors left the known for the unknown, survival skills surfaced to see us through those trying days.

Chapter 15
Keeping body and soul together...

When Singapore fell, our wonderful, fanciful rumors faded in the face of Japanese victories over the Pacific Rim. As reality set in, we knew that it was going to be a long haul of bare existence before liberation. Keeping body and soul together was clearly going to be, by necessity, a group effort. Fortunately, the "old know-how and can do" emerged into one of America's favorite pastimes: forming and appointing committees. Presbyterians from early America until today have delighted "in doing everything decently and in order" and that spirit permeated our struggle for survival. We had rice cleaners, kitchen crews, garbage collectors, ditch-cleaning crews, the Camp committee and teachers, women's committees, and hospital crews, just to name a few.

As the days wore on and groups came together for the common good, mining personnel and missionaries found a new respect for each other. At first, when allowed, the men had formed volleyball teams. They had divided themselves into missionaries and miners, known as Devil Chasers and Groundhogs, but as friendships formed, these divisions and names changed, and the teams were mixed.

Volleyball sounds frivolous in such a setting, but sports thrived, even though we were greatly diminished in energy and skill, providing a much needed relief from the daily drudgery. I remember with a great admiration when Roland Flory returned to camp after weeks of suffering and torture at the feared intelligence headquarters, and immediately after a short reunion with Jo and his new son, went out to the courts and joined in a game. A heroic effort to resume whatever normality still existed in camp.

By far, the most moving and uniting experience for us as a group was our first Easter celebration together. The Japanese, still high off their victory over Singapore, granted us the privilege of celebrating Easter together. It was to be a sunrise worship service on the tennis courts. Our tennis courts had become the equal of the traditional town square, where we were permitted occasionally to meet friends and family. Even during those times, we were separated by gender across a seven foot dividing line painted by Japanese guards, and the rule was strictly enforced. Each day the men were marched there for daily roll call. Now at long last it was to become a place of worship.

I do not remember the details of that service, but I do remember the exhilarating feeling of singing Easter hymns, listening to the ancient story of resurrection and hope. Simply knowing that that very day Christians throughout the world were also celebrating with us was a huge source of strength. Though prisoners, we were free in spirit. Believers and non-believers were bound by a tradition (beginning with Paul and Silas singing in jail) that had endured war and catastrophe for centuries. Now, that tradition enriched us and gave us new hope that we could endure in the days ahead to the time of our liberation and the renewing of the life of freedom we had once known and for which we now so passionately longed. The lovely hills around Baguio echoed as we sang our hope, and for the first time we could hear church bells ringing. For that precious moment, we were at peace with one another.

That evening we were once again permitted on the tennis courts. The Japanese said husbands and wives could walk together. How we all looked forward to that hour. In the exhilaration of the moment, some of the women designed hats of wild imagination made from whatever material they possessed. Fifth Avenue Easter Parade reproduced in a Japanese internment camp! With some trepidation, the Japanese watched as we all walked and talked intimately, laughing with our spouses for the first time since our imprisonment.

One of the rules was that we were only to be with our own husbands. Having "affairs" with someone else was not to be allowed. One of the very nervous guards, in the face of our exuberant actions, spotted a couple whose husband looked older than his wife. The guard jumped to the silly conclusion that they were not husband and wife. He stopped them by banging his rifle on the ground. Everyone was startled. Finally, with help from our camp officials, the guard calmed down, and we resumed our visit, but with a much more subdued attitude.

Every day, in one way or another, we were reminded that we were the defeated and imprisoned, and they were the conquerors. Today, those of us who experienced this, know and can imagine the terror the Serbs are inflicting on the Bosnians. And as we daily watch events unfold for these sad captives, we feel some of that helpless feeling of captivity once again. When are we ever going to learn the lessons of the past? Even as I write these words, the Allied Forces are conferring on bombing extensively the Serbian strongholds and a possible war involving us again in stupidity and horror.

I remember one time at Camp Holmes, the Mathers, Ed, and I were sitting on the bench Ed had built, overlooking the lovely valley that swept down to the China Sea. We were talking about the course of the war and inevitably, what was going on in the United States. Bruce said with conviction that there was one thing the government was working on: how to end the war and plan for the peaceful years ahead.

Surely, he felt, never again could a global war be spawned. I'm sure the ordinary people the world over were united in this thought whether friend or enemy. Since the end of "our war" there have been atrocities, small wars (only small if you weren't in them), and now the ancient rivalries of the Balkan states are in the thoughts of all of us. Thinking of grandchildren, our prayers are still constantly a yearning for peace.

After the fall of Bataan on April 10, the Japanese used the slogan "The Orient for Orientals," which crushed our spirits even more, for these events were on Philippine shores with our own men. They were defeated, dying, and discouraged beyond belief if they survived. While we lived with hunger and scarcity as our constant companions, our troops existed in cramped, crude quarters going through one of the most hellish, depraved experiences of the war.

A few of the women in camp had husbands in the military, both American and British. Alone and concerned about their husbands and their fates, they lived not knowing through the years of internment whether they had survived or died. Of all the women in our camp, these were the most courageous. At least most of us knew our husbands were in nearby barracks and had some method of daily communications with them throughout our internment.

Their pluck was typified by one of the British women who, mid-internment, was given the news through the International Red Cross that her husband had been wounded,. One day in conversation she exclaimed, "Well, I hope he wasn't hit in the hip where the hip pocket was because he always carried a Jewish Harp there. If that happened, his hip probably gives out musical notes as he walks!"

I remember, on our own return, talking with a friend and laughing about some camp experience. She coldly replied, "I don't see how you can laugh about such things." Well, laugh we did, and it was our sometimes strange sense of humor that got us through some very bad times.

Chapter 16
War never makes sense...

Perhaps this is the time to express my feelings of our survival. In our own camp, among the cool, lovely mountains of Northern Luzon, though we suffered hunger, the loss of some to death, saw others decline in health and strength, and had members of our community tortured, we, of all camps, were most fortunate. I remember Jim Halsema in one of his daily news sheets referring to our camp as the "Country Club of Internment Camps." We were a population of around five hundred compared to other civilian camps which contained thousands. For the most part, our population was well-educated and had skills that enabled us to survive, at times with a certain bravado.

Albert Einstein once was asked if he believed in miracles. He replied, "All of life is a miracle!" To paraphrase that, we could say, "In our internment situation, all of survival was a miracle." Certainly we experienced circumstances which make it seem a true miracle that we survived. These times were sobering as we rejoiced in our survival after some harrowing instances. But such thoughts are even more sobering when we think of those who did not survive; those who never experienced the exhilaration of rescue and release.

When we returned to the United States, some said, "You came home because you were in our prayers." What a troublesome bit of theology that was because countless others, who were also prayed for, did not come home. Even today, all over the world, people suffer and die without a miracle coming their way.

How can a person without the hope that adequate food and shelter will be supplied, pray, "Give us this day our daily bread"? Such questions have been with us for centuries--baffling sages, philosophers and theologians.

I remember a story in a woman's magazine in the early sixties. It was about world leaders who, in the midst of possible immediate annihilation, gathered together in Geneva. All the ideals, philosophies, religions were put in a computer to solve the problems of achieving lasting world peace. Destruction seemed imminent. Tensely they waited for the solution to be spewed out of the computer. Finally, the solution printed out to be read by the group. It was handed to the President of the United States to be read to the assembled personage. He first read it to himself, then hopelessly put his head on the table and wept in despair. The message was "Love your neighbors as yourself." Five words and we still have been unable to accomplish it.

When possible, the Filipinos smuggled in notes to us with news. When it could be arranged, loans were also made. The Filipinos purchased food and sent it in to us. There was constant danger in these actions, and I wonder if the situations were reversed and the risks similar, if we would have responded as bravely. All over the islands, Filipinos were suffering unspeakably: losing lives, homes, and businesses. Guerilla activity among them continued.

War never makes sense, so why does human kind continue to think it ever solves anything? Eventually we must come to the negotiating table and work things out peaceably. We do not seem to possess the wisdom or skill to do this before a war begins.

Occasionally, there are glimmers of hope that negotiations might work. But on this very day, August 23, 1995, three of our diplomats were brought home for burial due to an accident in the Serb-Croat-Bosnia war because they were not allowed to use the safer, preferred place of negotiation. The history of this conflict has lasted for centuries.

I remember when one of our churches sponsored a Yugoslavian-Bulgarian refugee family. On the first Sunday they came to church with us. Afterward, we told them they were free to go to the church of their choice. There was a Greek Orthodox Church in nearby Dayton, and we told them that we could arrange for them to attend there since they were of the Orthodox faith. That really brought a heated response. They said eight hundred years ago Greeks raided across the borders, destroying a church, killing those who occupied it. There was no way they could attend a church with such people. Later, they moved to Cleveland where the husband had a job in an automobile plant and we visited them there. The husband sheepishly said there were Greeks employed at the factory with whom he had to work. To his surprise, he found out that they were pretty good fellows.

Occasionally, such contact with our guards left us with some of the same emotions. One such incident occurred while we were still in Camp John Hay. Several of the guards were tramping noisily through the woman's barracks one night, when one of the guards yelled at a woman with a small child and an infant to keep her children from crying. Obviously, that was easier said than done in a crowded, strange sleeping area with snoring neighbors and creaking floors. As the other guard passed the apprehensive mother, he picked up the baby and walked with it until the baby calmed down and the mother was able to comfort the older child. At first, the mom was uneasy with the guard picking up the baby, but she soon relaxed when she saw his intent. Perhaps he, too, had a heavy heart and a family in Japan for whom he longed and this gave him a moment of peace. Perhaps, if the entire world could only hold each other's babies, our feelings toward those unlike us would change.

Chapter 17
...deep yearnings for freedom.

Soon after our first Easter in internment, we received notice that we were being moved to Camp Holmes, a Filipino constabulary camp a few miles from Baguio. To a captive civilian group change by military orders is always unnerving. We wondered what their motives and reasoning's were, but having no choice, planning began for the tremendous task packing our meager belongings, and facing inevitable change, again.

The Japanese allowed some of our men to go ahead by a few days to clean and arrange for our move, which included cleaning a primitive kitchen that already existed. As I remember it, the stoves had huge cauldrons inserted deep into wood stoves where eventually our daily rice was cooked, stews (sometimes of doubtful contents) were made and some amazingly good meals on special holidays were prepared. These were overseen by our very gifted chef, Alec Kalusny. Upon our release, he was employed by Trader Vics in San Francisco. How fortunate we were...In spite of rumors of "kitchen graft" by the food crew, we owed a great deal to them for their ability, in less than ideal circumstances, to prepare three meals a day for the three years of our internment.

By the time the actual move was made, it was a worn out, tired, and apprehensive group that drove out to Camp Holmes. I remember the first night, just laying my mattress down and collapsing with Carol in my arms for a night of restless sleep.

The next few days of "settling in" are rather vague in my memory. There were three large barracks on what came to be known as "topside." Beneath that, the land sloped steeply down towards a large house, which was used as a makeshift hospital, and two smaller officer bungalows, one of which became the infamous "pampered Baby House." The other house was used as a high school building. From

Carol's + Helen's Cubicle 8'x5'

Helen and Carol's cubicle in the baby house.

the vantage point of the baby house, spread a magnificent, lovely view of Trinidad Valley. On a clear day we had a tantalizing view of the China Sea. This view fed our souls as we gazed at the valley below, but as one grumpy realist said, "But you can't eat it!" Regardless, it was a continued source of mental and spiritual refreshment, barbed wire fence notwithstanding.

Perhaps I should explain my statement of "the infamous Baby House." In the early days of our move to Camp Holmes, at the ruling of the camp committee, the youngest babies and their mothers were assigned to the Baby House. I imagine that they also had the motive of saving the internees in the "topside" barracks from having to submit to the crying of twelve or more infants during the nights and days, only adding to the confusion, which was already in full and constant swing.

Those of us who were permitted to live there with the youngest of babies were privileged. Since most of us were young missionaries from China, just starting our families before the war began it was somewhat of a "double whammy" to the reputation of those living there. Some were delighted to find us committing any sort of transgression. There was one internee who gleefully asked

View from Camp Holmes to the China Sea.

me, "If cleanliness is next to godliness, how come I saw a missionary with a dirty neck?" Immediately the back of my neck began to crawl, and I asked myself, "Is it I, Lord?" Fortunately, it wasn't as I checked immediately upon her departure.

As to the "Baby House," being a four room cottage, we were just as crowded, but admittedly, it was a less

79

Road past Camp Holmes.

Men's barracks at Camp Holmes.

confusing place than living "topside." Another plus was
that we missed the minor feuds and disagreements, fueled
by living in larger, nosier, and more confined quarters.
Therefore, we were looked upon with some envy and
prejudice.   However, for the most part, with the differences
in backgrounds and beliefs, camp fared remarkably well in
"the business of getting along."

  In the beginning, one of the touchiest subjects at Camp
Holmes was that the men's committee had decided that
only men could vote in camp as this was wartime and what
did women know about that? Well, we knew almost as
much as the men as not many of them were well versed in
war either. Especially the single women felt left out as they
did not have husbands that they could try to sway to their
thinking.
  Consequently, we had to go through the whole suffrage
thing again. A short, vigorous, and successful campaign
was waged, and we were allowed to vote! Though several

Sterilizing shed for camp hospital.

Camp Holmes.

political factions flourished at times, for the most part we had a pretty democratic "go" at it. The Japanese, with strong prompting from the committee, allowed us to form our own governing process, and the committees served us ably and well, despite the usual disagreements bound to exist in any society.

Each of us had our own deep yearnings for freedom. The constant lack of privacy, the ever present noise, the uncertainty of each day, worries about adequate food supplies, and the inevitable "turn over" of the military were just some of our concerns.

But everything is relative. I became friends with one of the Catholic nuns when we were both confined in the camp hospital with dysentery. The sides of our cots touched their full length so becoming "close friends" was inevitable. One day she said to me, "You people in camp feel confined and imprisoned, but to us cloistered nuns, this is the first freedom we have had in a long time." They were a great addition to our camp, helping in many ways. When she was transferred to Manila, I received from her several beautifully embroidered baby dresses for Carol.

Chapter 18
...an R and R situation.

Each day seemed to bring new problems between guards, Japanese officers, and internees. For the most part, diplomacy, patience, and a sense of humor prevailed. One such instance happened when a bare light bulb was dangling from the women's barracks' ceiling near a window. It swayed back and forth and in doing so, the bulb would go on and off, obviously a short. However, one of the guards saw it blink on and off, and thought someone was signaling to the Filipino guerrillas in the surrounding hills. He was beside himself with anger, and fear, I suppose. After a great deal of ranting and raving, he finally calmed down. Our daily lives and safety depended on such minor instances.

At our last reunion in Los Angeles, Fred Crouter, better known as "Bedie," told this tale of an encounter with a Japanese guard. When the boys living in the barracks with their mothers turned twelve years old, they were required to move to the men's barracks with their dads. During the day, the boys were allowed their moms in the barracks.

One time Fred was particularly "down" and visited his mom's cubicle. Time slipped by and he suddenly realized that it was way past the time when he should have returned to his dad. It was dark outside and it was "lights out" inside the barracks also. He crept down the darkened, wooden stairs, and there at the bottom was one of the dreaded Japanese guards. The guard thrust his rifle on to the ground. Fred thought all was lost. Shaking, he looked at the guard, who stretched out his hand and placed a yo-yo in his hand!

I think our camp was looked upon by the Japanese as almost as R and R situation. Every three months the guards were changed, because the Japanese feared that if they stayed too long the guards would get too friendly and more lenient. When the old guards left, they were replaced by new ones, fresh from active duty and full of hate and anger toward us, the enemy. Those first few days of "changing of the guards" were always a tense time. We all toed the line and hoped for the best when such a change took place.

Japanese and Americans did however have a common love, baseball. Occasionally, officers would come from Baguio and want to play. Our men would hastily get a team together. Then fear would enter the hearts of our team--should our men beat the Japanese officers or let them win?

One of the Episcopal men interned with us had lived in Tokyo. There he had faithfully attended Japanese baseball games. One of the officers recognized him in camp, and because of their mutual love of the game and attendance in Tokyo, he was released. Too bad we weren't all able to be that farsighted.

Chapter 19
When will it cease?

One of the drawbacks to being interned on an island is that there are not any friendly borders across which to escape if the opportunity arises. In addition, since we were of different skin color, we would have been instantly recognized. The indignity for our men of being prisoners was surely harder on their egos than the women's, even though our pride and egos became bruised and shafted many times. Ironically, the obstacles to successful escape allowed those in camp to relinquish such ideas, and we were indirectly spared further indignities by angry Japanese.

Two of our single men did successfully escape. They had connections to guerrilla activity as the war neared its end. The results of just two escaping wrought instant anxiety, torture, lessening of privileges, and the erections of more fences around our camp. Because of it, our one outstanding Commandant, Mr. Tomibe, was removed and punished. We all suffered from his departure. Because of the threat made in the beginning of our internment of killing ten men for every escapee, three men in our camp offered to be in that number. One was a man who had served in the Boxer Rebellion in Peking many years ago. He felt, because of his age and not having many more years to live, that he should be one of those. Another was a man from Australia who was suffering from a brain tumor and knew his days were also numbered. Fortunately, this threat had been forgotten, but we had some tense hours wondering if it would be enforced.

As I write this I realize how memory fails after fifty-some years, and how minute details of camp experiences have faded. To learn of the details of this experience and other problems of camp experience, read Natalie Crouter's book <u>Forbidden Diary</u>. In it are details of our common experience of politics, pettiness, nobleness, pleasures, and anguish in the midst of the devastation of war.

The insight and knowledge gained during our internment has given our lives the direction needed to better understand and accept ideas from other religions and races, and strive toward things better for the human condition in the years to come. "Without a vision, the people perish." May this not be the fate of our human existence.

Fred Crouter and his sister June, were two of my favorite teens in camp. Fred later remembered that whenever he was about to do something questionable, there was always an adult snaking out an arm to his shoulder and saying, "We don't do that." The old African concept of "it takes a village to raise a child" certainly existed in camp. Now, often the intimate, familiar village is gone. Both parents usually have to work, ethics are prevented from being taught in school, and teens cluster together for "security" in gangs. No wonder we all feel adrift, bewildered and frightened for what is to come.

Churches do not reach out enough to all kids. I remember one pastor in Chicago answering a parishioner's criticism of damage to the interior of the church in their sponsored youth activities, "I'd rather the inside of the church gets messed up than the outside have rocks thrown at it."

Not withstanding the extremes of the Christian right, we must admit our lack of spirituality and ability to share it in society today. We are the most giving of nations monetarily, but we need to share more aggressively the ideas that motivate that giving. Camp life in a far away island conquered by a feared enemy seems almost a haven now, as we search ways for successful daily existence with our friends and enemies.

Chapter 20
Food was the main topic of conversation

All of us had camp jobs. For a time, Ed was involved with the hospital. Each day he and "Gibby" washed and sterilized the hospital laundry in large garbage cans over a hot wood fire in a lean-to-shelter, just outside the hospital. They stirred the linens with large wooden sticks and then hung them to dry. It was hot and repulsive work but a vital, and necessary task.

(Phyllis Gibbons, known to most as "Gibby" was from England, and during World War I, she had entertained the troops by playing the piano and singing. During our weekly Saturday night entertainment time, she led the camp in singing popular, nostalgic songs as she played our old, beat-up camp piano. One night when the heavy, old upright was not in the position she desired, she rose up and moved it all by herself to a more suitable place. She was a strong, independent and often funny lady. Later, she was a tutor in Japan to General MacArthur's son.)

By far, the most time consuming job was sorting the rice. Every day, we spread the rice out on long tables in the main dining room, and in shifts picked out weevils and other debris. One of the camp's mottoes was "See no weevil, hear no weevil and eat no weevil!" Hearing them was not a joke. Toward the last days of our internment in Baguio, the Baby House inhabitants were moved "topside" to a building which had been used as storage for the camp. In it was still one room filled with rice and cornmeal. At night when all was quiet, you could hear those busy little weevils crunching away on our reserves. They were like a foraging enemy army, destroying our food supply.

Food was the main topic of conversation whenever we got together. People collected recipes from one another as Elizabeth Taylor collected diamonds. Each recipe was considered a gem, and we duly expected to try them out on our return to the United States. While we were pretty good at adapting recipes to the food at hand in camp, I remember some saying that as soon as they got home they were going to buy a cow for it meant milk and meat, two things longed for in those barren days.

In addition to the daily, organized camp cooking, there was also "Private Cooking." Where it got the name "private" I don't know. Nothing was "private," especially cooking, as our little improvised "tin can" pots of goodies simmering away were scrutinized and diagnosed as to what "so and so" had managed to obtain. If you didn't stay at the small stove, your stuff inevitably got pushed to the back where it was less hot.

It would be difficult to list or even remember all the substitutions we made in our private cooking. Recently Betty Foley gave me a cake recipe which was typical of the substitutions made in original recipes:

<u>Mrs. Gowan's Recipe for Chocolate Cake</u>

1 1/2 cup Cassava flour
1 cup rice flour
1 tsp. coconut oil
1 small panoche ball (raw sugar boiled down into a ball, sometimes with bugs which had to be strained out)
1 tsp. salt
1 or 2 native eggs
1 cup soy bean milk (made in camp)
Small amount of velvet bean (carob)

<u>Directions:</u>
--If no cassava flour is available, use all rice flour but add two mashed bananas to hold mix together.
--Leave out the bean milk and add 1 tsp of pineapple vinegar or calamenci juice.
--Eggs may be left out but add two extra bananas.
--If no fat of any kind is available, add Abolene face cream. It will work but is not very rich.
--When soy bean milk is not available, water may be used but add a little vinegar or calamenci juice.

<u>Caution:</u> Do not use too much velvet bean as a little gives a fair chocolate flavor. Too much makes it bitter. Don't use cassava flour as mixture will be rubbery.

--In case of no fat, no sugar or no eggs, mixture may be steamed in tin can for brown bread. In which case, substitute corn flour for Cassava flour.

--If this mix does not rise properly or is gummy, add a little corn beef (from Red Cross package) and garlic. Bake it for spoon bread.

I guess an explanation of Aboline face cream is needed at this point. I was fortunate to have some, for when we left for China, my mother gave me a large can of Aboline. She said it was "always nice to have." She said actresses used it to remove make up as it was so inexpensive. I packed it away, but never used it until our former landlord in Baguio sent it in with a few things.   Little did my mother know that it would come in handy as a cooking oil. It contained no fragrance and, hopefully no other harmful ingredients.

The soybean milk mentioned in the recipe was originally developed by our Church of the Brethren doctor, Lloyd Cunningham. He had gone to Loma Linda Medical School, a Seventh Day Adventist institution. The SDAs are known for their knowledge of good nutrition, and since some of them were also interned, they and Lloyd worked out a recipe for baby formula. Using the hospital autoclave as a pressure cooker, they cooked the tough soybeans. It was an unappetizing, gray, slimy mass without much resemblance to milk, and we had to enlarge the nipple holes to allow the concoction to flow through, but for the most part, the babies adapted to it. Sometimes we were able to get small amounts of caribou milk into camp, but the source was never reliable.

At one point the camp bought a number of goats, in the hopes that they would provide a constant milk supply. That effort proved to me that while in theory communism was great, in reality it was problematic. Several men were assigned the task of goat herding. To most of them, it was just a job, and a rather pesky one at that for goats are not the most amenable animals known to mankind. Therefore,

Goat herder for camp goats.

91

the goats did not thrive, and the milk supply continued to
be scarce. At that point they allowed each of us with a
baby to have a goat and the fathers cared for them.
Because it was to their own child's benefit to have the milk,
great care was taken and the milk did increase some.
There is nothing like personal pride and incentive in doing
a good job.

The goat we received was sickly and produced almost
no milk, so we finally had to butcher it and eat the meat.
While we had carefully boiled the milk for Carol, we did
handle the raw meat with bare hands. Undulant fever was
endemic in the Philippines, and that is where I probably
contracted the undulant fever that was later diagnosed in
the United States and prevented us from going to Ecuador
a year after our return. One of the blood tests done when I
had jaundice in camp showed that I had some unknown
infection. Dr. Haughwout had examined the blood sample,
but was unable to diagnose it with the simple equipment
that he had at camp. He advised me to check it out after
we arrived home.

(The Cleveland Clinic made the diagnosis. Fortunately,
when we moved to Muncie, Indiana, there was a doctor in a
nearby town who was an authority on the fever. He gave
me the new, expensive drug Aureomycin which took care of
the problem. During camp I had felt extreme tiredness but
just thought it was due to poor nutrition. Fortunately, I
had not contracted it until after I had stopped nursing
Carol or I would have infected her as well. The clinic
suggested that I stay in the United States for at least five
years; just to be sure it was under control. Thus, our
missionary career came to an end.)

Carol was fortunate enough to have been born in the
first few weeks of our internment, before the lack of a
proper diet would have affected her, and she remained
amazingly well, considering the conditions in which we
lived. I kept a record of her early diet. At two and a half
months, her first solid foods were cereal and tomato juice.
At three months she had mashed bananas. At six months
camotes (yams), carrots, papaya, squash, eggs
occasionally, rhubarb, bean milk, and beef broth. On

August 18, 1942, she ate half of a ten centavo in paper money. I still have the other half that I dug out of her mouth.

One of Carol's favorite snacks were small, dried fish, called dilly fish. They were only about an inch and a half long, and they were dried whole, bulgy, beady eyes and all. I reheated them and put them on her chair tray for her to eat. She enjoyed them much more than the rest of us did. Years later when she had her teeth straightened, the orthodontist said she was a year behind in her bone structure development. So much for dilly fish being a source of protein and calcium. She did have a bout of dysentery, which sent her to the hospital for several days. It was heart breaking to see her go, but we knew she was in the best of hands. The volunteer doctors and nurses were such a dedicated and loving group of people. The entire camp owes them a great deal..

Coffee was held in high regard in camp because it was a stimulating source of pleasure, in an otherwise drab, monotonous, and lean diet. Unfortunately, coffee also was affected by supply and demand. On Sundays, if obtainable, there was fresh brewed coffee for our camp breakfast. Mondays and Tuesdays the same grounds were used. On Wednesday, the cooks added a small amount of fresh grounds to aid the depleted brew. This lasted through Thursday, Friday, and Saturday, and on Sunday the process began again.

One of the Seventh Day Adventists by the name of Frost invented a coffee by burning corn and grinding the scorched kernels. This was dubbed "Frostina" and added some rather doubtful variety to our camp menu.

We did, at times, have small gardens, but the scarcity of seeds, tools, and energy severely limited this endeavor. On one occasion, our family of three was issued 15 peanuts. After some discussion we decided to plant them and hope that a larger amount would grow. They were just beginning to sprout when the Japanese ordered the Baby House occupants to move "topside." We tried to transplant them, but it was too much for our fifteen peanuts.

During the last year of the war, the Japanese permitted us to plant a camp garden on one of the nearby hillsides.

Chow Line

Rolland Flory helped direct this, as he was an agricultural missionary. One of his ideas was to create a makeshift irrigation system out of bamboo poles. This system worked well, and provided us with camotes (yams), a tough but much needed source of vitamins.

Also, to aid our food supply, we were permitted to have a camp store, located in a lean-to. Sporadically, food was brought in to sell, and internees used whatever small amount they had available to supplement our meager diets. However, things were very expensive, and it was of very little use to those of us who had hardly any cash.

The one glorious event that stands out for all the internees was the arrival of the Red Cross food packages, clothing and medical supplies. Actually, according to Geneva Convention rules, each prisoner was to have one food box every month, but during the more than three years that we were there, we received one package apiece.

Maintaining a steady flow of food and other supplies is one of the problems of being interned in wartime on an island. Those of us who were interned, at least had a trickle of food brought to us by the Japanese, regardless of its quality or scarcity. They did not abide by the Geneva Convention for POWs, but food was supplied, full of weevils, and sometimes spoiled, but it kept us alive.

However, the Filipinos had no such steady resources to draw upon. It was all up to their individual ingenuity and enterprise to raise and garner whatever supplies they could, and every day was an agonizing struggle. Japanese surveillance and harassment were their constant

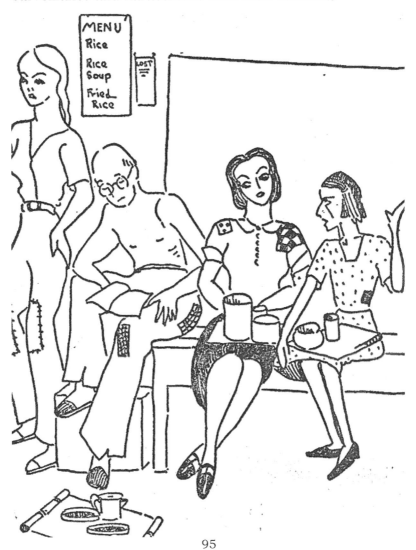

MENU
Rice
Rice Soup
Fried Rice

LOST

" Private " Cooking

companions during these times. Yet in spite of all this,
they took risks and made sacrifices to send those in camp
a supply of food whenever permitted by the Japanese.
Those of us who were new to the Islands, were sporadically
sent in food bought with money borrowed from outside
sources. Occasionally, Filipino church members or former
landlords would send in packages.

(Borrowing fifty pesos once, after the war we were given
a bill through the Church for an amount increased to an
exorbitant price above the fifty pesos. We were charged

$1500 in American dollars. We were never quite sure of the source of the loan, but Ed paid it. Our thinking was that we had survived, while others had lost far more than this in possessions, homes, and life savings, to say nothing of physical suffering and death.

Chapter 21
Repairing and laundering clothing...

After solving the most important problems of existing and procuring sufficient food for the five hundred "guests of the Japanese Imperial Army and Emperor," we had to devise a way to mend, repair and launder clothing brought into camp. Fortunately, the climate, except during the rainy season, was mild.

I had come in with mostly maternity clothes. Usually expectant moms are anxious to rid themselves of voluminous maternity dresses, but we wore them for several more years with minor alterations. One of my outfits had a matching jacket, and when Carol was about a year old, I made a dress for her out of the jacket, sewing it by hand. Lucy Vinson remarked that she bet not many kids wore the same clothes before and after they were born!

As the men's trousers became worn, they became shorts, or what is now known as "cut-offs." The material from the lower trouser leg was used to patch the remaining garment or to make skirts for the wives. This was a trick women used in the Depression of the thirties. They would split the worn trouser legs into two pieces, one from each leg, turned the worn material inside out and made an A-line skirt.

As shirts wore out, the men wore no tops as they performed hard, manual tasks in the camp. I suppose with beards, poor haircuts, and scrounged clothing, we were harbingers of the kids of the hippie era! When Ed came home he found it difficult to wear the necessary tee shirt when he was gardening. He yearned for the "good old days," just like the ancient Jews yearned for the garlic in the days of their captivity in Egypt.

As shoes wore out, the men in the shop patched them with pieces of old, worn-out tires. This created a new style, for below the uppers, "fringe" developed at the edges of the cut tire soles. After the uppers were gone, wooden clogs were fashioned and held on by strips of old inner tubes.

With the wire from inside the tires, the men on "shop duty" made hair pins, hair fasteners, and other useful things. Bill Junkin took some of the wire and fashioned egg beaters for his and Jessie's friends at Christmas. He circled the wire in a receding spiral. The narrow end he inserted into a wooden handle. On the flat front side of the handles, he embedded wire in the shape of the recipient's last initial. How's that for luxury--a monogrammed egg beater? The bigger luxury was getting eggs to beat!

Sewing materials were also extremely scarce. One woman had brought in a handmade quilt, so whenever she needed thread for mending, she would carefully "unquilt" the quilt for the thread.

I learned to knit in camp. One of the men made knitting needles of various sizes of bamboo. Ed's mother had made and sent him a sweater which did not fit, so I ripped it out, split the four-ply yarn into 2-ply yarn, and I started to re-knit the sweater. We had to make our own patterns with the help of an expert knitter. I worked on that for a long time, thinking how great it would be for him to have a sweater during the damp, chilly, rainy season. I finished it just as we were being moved to Bilibid prison in humid Manila. We could only take a limited amount of luggage with us, and we left the bulky sweater behind. I've always hoped that a Filipino found it.

As the men's underwear wore out, they resorted to wearing a Japanese type called a fundoshi. They were similar to a G-string with material between their legs. Bras for women were a problem as they were patched, repatched, and finally abandoned. I made a bra by carefully ripping my remaining worn-out one apart and using those pieces for a pattern. No "twenty-four-hour-bras" for us with a tempting uplift. We had 'em for twenty-four months or more and forget the uplift. For most of us, there wasn't much to lift anyway.

Before the war, in Baguio, there had been a women's Monday Club. They sewed and clothed needy Filipinos. Shortly after our internment, materials and clothing came in from the Club's supply. Ironically, some of the women

Bathtime for Little Jailbirds ...

got to wear the clothes they had made for the Filipinos. Extra material was given out to people as their prewar clothes became unwearable. As an extra volunteer job, several talented women had the task of making patterns for various pieces of clothing.

Feminine needs in camp became an acute problem as the supply of Kotex from town dwindled. Once again, I was fortunate for my mother had insisted that I buy a forty-yard package of cotton cheese cloth, saying, "You never know." How right she was. I divided the forty yards into four sections and shared with close friends.

Laundering was another problem. Soap was extremely scarce and sometimes nonexistent. Some of the men, when they showered, would leave their underwear on, washing their body and clothes at one time. It also saved on scarce water. Ecology at its very best.

For some time, Ed and I had bars of Ivory soap. Before we sailed from Vancouver, I had purchased a crate of Ivory soap which was on sale. It contained 36 bars. When we were in our stateroom, I moved the bars from the box to the steamer trunk, using all the nooks and crannies left in our luggage. We never used them in Peking, but while we were in Camp Holmes our landlord sent them in a package. As our precious supply of soap ran out, some was available in our little store and some poor quality soap was made in camp.

There were times when most of us were completely without any. So, we sloshed clothes and diapers, and hung them in the sun, hoping the sun would do its work. During the rainy season, when it was impossible to hang things outside, this proved to be a real problem for the Baby House which housed ten or eleven babies. We had a very small kitchen with a wood burning stove, so we strung lines back and forth, and each mother was allowed to hang diapers for a certain length of time. Fortunately, it was cool during the rainy season, and the stove usually gave off enough heat to dry them in the allotted time. Cooking in the kitchen, while dodging rows of wet diapers, was quite an acquired art.

Airing out blankets and mattresses was another job that went on constantly. The camp was kept quite clean for so many people living in such close quarters. The early fears of running short of water never occurred for which we felt most fortunate.

The rainy season was always an ordeal, but here again we were fortunate to be in the mountains. In Baguio, it never simply rained; it was always a torrential deluge. Baguio has one of the heaviest rainfalls in the world. Fortunately, most of it drained off the mountainsides rather quickly. At these times, we were forced to stay indoors, and people's irritability rose accordingly. We always strove to cope with overcrowding, especially important during these times. Unfortunately for those in the barracks, the "private" cooking was done outdoors with our small, wood-burning stove between the barracks. It only had a roof-top shelter, so typhoon winds and rain kept this activity at a minimum. Just one more frustration added to an already constricted existence.

One of the most memorable times of "stormy weather" was at the tail end of a fierce typhoon that swept the Philippines when the small Baby House almost lost its roof. We could hear it ominously raising up and banging down again. The fathers, who were then at "topside," were allowed to come down. Equipped with heavy ropes, they strapped them around the rafters. As the typhoon's fury lifted the roof, the men clung desperately. The wind lifted them and the roof off the ground. Fortunately, they did not take off across the valley, but were jolted down to the floor of the attic by their combined weight each time. There were frightful thuds to be heard, but they literally "hung in there" and saved the roof. I remember them coming down wet, exhausted, but triumphant, having "saved the day," or rather the night, filled with primitive, macho delight at being the heroes of the hour.

Chapter 22
...life-saving food, clothing, and medicine.

During the Christmas season in 1943, we received our one shipment of Red Cross packages and other supplies by a very circuitous, involved route. We only received this because our Japanese commandant, Mr. Tomibe, was determined to see that this shipment reach our camp. Some of our men, Carl Eshbach among them, were sent to Manila with Mr. Tomibe to receive and guard the shipment of life-saving food, clothing, and medicine. After its arrival in our camp, it was stored in the Bodega at the edge of our camp. Once there, trusted Americans and Japanese guards diligently guarded and supervised the distribution of the precious shipment. In our malnourished condition, it boggled our minds' knowing that this much good was nearby and would soon be in our possession. Excitement ruled the days that followed the shipment's arrival.

We had been told the contents of each box and planning immediately filled our minds. Powdered milk, cigarettes, Spam, and chocolate were among the most coveted contents. After receiving the boxes, one for each person, swapping became the main activity.

Smokers were the most avid in their search for someone who would swap their cigarettes for something from the smoker's box. I remember Bessie refused to swap her cigarettes, as she believed that it was wrong to smoke. She endured all kinds of pressure. Dr. Nance tried to convince her that it certainly was O.K. as the Pennsylvania Dutch, from whence came the Church of the Brethren, were actually raising tobacco, but Bessie held fast.

The rest of the missionaries, especially those with children, did not have a problem swapping our cigarettes for powdered milk or other nourishing cans of food. Dr. Haoughwart, who had taken a liking to Ed, gave us a can of powdered milk for Carol, simply as a gift. We felt humbled and grateful at such a show of friendship. It was interesting to note how various people reacted to our newly received treasures.

Even though we were entitled to a Red Cross box every month, the boxes were only given to us that one time. Had we received boxes monthly, the many future health problems may have been averted. One of our friends took his cans out each week, reveling at the contents, and carefully polished each can. Some of the internees dived into the wonderful goodies, others rationed them carefully. Most of us saved a portion for "the turnover," when conditions would surely be chaotic.

Clothing was also sent. Each woman received a pastel, sateen "play suit," consisting of one-piece-shirt and shorts combined with an over skirt. Someone remarked that we looked like a girl's camp in uniform. Just having something that was not patched or faded helped our feminine pride immensely. We trimmed or embroidered them to give a little individuality. I monogrammed mine with an "H" on the blouse pocket.

Carol received an outfit of play clothing that was nice enough to wear after our return to the United States. I remember a friend, when she saw what Carol was wearing, remarked that she had made identical clothing for the Red Cross. When I told her that this was Red Cross, she was shocked that she knew someone, who at one time had needed such assistance. It was difficult for people to relate to our being prisoners-of-war. They could not understand why we did not view "our experience" as evil, and filled with terror.

By now it was late 1943, and our release did not come until early 1945. At this time in Camp Holmes, everything was scarce and getting scarcer. Our caches of food slowly disappeared, despite resolutions to save them. Had it not been for that one shipment, our plight would have been much more serious. Besides receiving actual nourishment, it was a real boost in our morale to know that we had not been forgotten.

Chapter 23
What dreamers we were...

At these times more than others, classes flourished. Many talented people were in camp and were more than willing to share their creativity and knowledge. Nellie McKim taught Japanese flower arrangements, and Dr. Bergaminie, the architect from Tokyo, taught us how to do architectural drawings for dream houses. There were a variety of language classes, oral readings of Shakespeare, and Bible study groups. All of these and more were taught with scarce supplies, but an abundance of imagination. Reading was at a minimum because very few books found their way into camp. The mainstay of our library was provided by the daring-do of Dr. Nance.

One day he had to go to the hospital on an errand in the old, black supply truck, manned by armed Japanese guards. For some reason on this particular trip, they made a stop at the Pines Hotel. Dr. Nance knew that in the lobby was a bookcase full of books so he grabbed a gunny sack, ran inside, swept all the books that he could into the sack, and brought our looted library into being. A small shack with shelves was erected and became the center of culture at Camp Holmes.

One of the most popular volumes was a shabby, worn Sears Roebuck catalog. It was checked out often. Internees poured over its pages of almost forgotten items, like glossy stoves, refrigerators filled with food, sets of dishes, radios, clothes and all the things deemed necessary in those lost days of pre-internment. Ed and I estimated that upon our release, with the prewar prices in the catalog, we could have the necessary appliances to set up housekeeping again for under two hundred dollars. What dreamers we were in those dreary, war torn, anxious days.

Chapter 24
..."man does not live by bread alone"...

There were some wonderful moments in our captivity. Some of the most outstanding were the pageants for Christmas and Easter, accompanied by a choir whose singing was honed to perfection by the capable church music directors interned with us. One Easter production, of the Crucifixion and Resurrection, was acted out in a beautiful rock garden below the Baby House. It was filmed by the Japanese to be shown in Japan to prove how well we were being treated. Actually, that was far from the truth, but served as great propaganda for the Japanese. That "man does not live by bread alone" was proven over and over again by the courage and strength received from these rare occasions.

One particularly moving experience was a high school production of <u>Our Town</u> by Thornton Wilder produced by Father Gowan, a dedicated English teacher from Brent School. Amazingly well done, we all felt a little homesick as we watched these wonderful kids recreate a moment in time in small town America. It was something that we could relate to with nostalgia for what once was. It was not an amateur production in any sense, compared with the average high school play. In our favor was the fact that we did not have to pay an exorbitant royalty and that they had a masterpiece to work with. Father Gowan mentioned this, hoping that Thornton Wilder would not try to collect after interment. But beyond that, it was a magical moment which true theater is. Those students are now grandparents, and probably do not realize the high regard in which we still hold memories of them so long ago. And so, "Thank you for the memory!"

Small ball-and-chain pins were made for each graduate. I believe that three classes graduated. Upon their return to the United States, not a single one was turned down for college entrance. They were all well-

Moms and children at Camp Holmes.

educated in the highest sense of the word, having had extremely dedicated, gifted teachers.

The students had their own school song, arranged by John Robinson with lyrics by Rev. Vincent Gowan:

Verse one:
We sing our Alma Mater.
We hope it won't be long
Before there's nothing left of her--
Except this fleeting song.

Verse two:
For ball and chain we're wearing,
Our teachers wear them too.
Our uniform is Sing-Sing stripes,
Our colors mostly blue.

Verse three:
And when we're back in freedom,
We'll not forget these days.
Upon our dingy classrooms,
We'll look with tearful gaze,

107

And see our mother school,
Camp Holmes, as through a golden haze.

A "golden haze" is not how many of our children now reflect on their education. It's a scary, doubtful experience for many, brand-name jeans withstanding. Those who studied while at Camp Holmes did so under the constant threat of hunger, poor clothing, and terror from war days, the constant presence of the enemy with guns and swords being evident a all times, and yet they succeeded.

With next to nothing in equipment and supplies, students sat upon their forbidden history books when a guard approached the school room, for the class supposedly being taught was English II. These teenagers did not have radios, T.V's, boom boxes, cars, extravagant sports programs, bands, or prom nights. They labored under the threat of a long, drawn-out war and their doubtful-chance-of-survival, and they did so with flying colors. Perhaps present day administrators, teachers and parents could find some answers they so desperately need by studying this group.

During the three years that we were at Camp Holmes, people's creative juices flowed through the Saturday night entertainment, pageants, and plays, even in this most barren of existence. Most engaged in "creating" in the best sense of the word. If we are created in God's image, certainly the ability to create is inherent in most people. And so it was at Camp Holmes during our internment.

We created, saw "that it was good." and held an exhibit of things we had made in the two years of internment to that point in time. Even the Japanese guards attended our exhibits, and showed their appreciation for our varied and ingenious objects.

The use of materials was limited, but varied. Objects made of coconut shell were in great abundance: bowls, bracelets, pins and necklaces. We had at our disposal the older dark brown coconut shell and the lighter shell of newer coconuts--inlaid work, light superimposed on dark, highly polished things of delight.

Ed made me an oval brooch of dark coconut on top of which was a light shell carved in the shape of a Chinese junk. He also made a small round dark pin for Carol with her initial "C" carved in the light shell. I swapped one of my water colors for someone to cut out our Chinese name of peace made of coconut. The character consisted of a roof under which was a stylized figure of a woman. (Incidentally, the word for "trouble" is two women under one roof.) I attached it to a braided yarn about six inches long with a tassel and used it as a bookmark.

Wayne Miller made a beautiful, leather-bound box for his wife, Bunny. He owned an old, gold-edged leather-bound book, and glued all the pages together until they formed a firm rectangular block. Then he carefully sawed a rectangular hole in the glued paper, leaving narrow edges all around for the edges of the box, and glued the back binding to the hollowed out block. The front of the book served as a lid. It was a richly bound leather box when finished.

Containers were highly treasured and shown off with pride. The men in the shop made coffee pots from old cans. The lid knobs and the pots' welded-on handles were well shaped. One of the stories that Jim Halsema tells in his memoirs is of two shop men talking about all the work that they did for camp internees. One said, "I've made a number of coffee pots for the women and not one has offered me a cup of coffee." The other man replied saying, "Well, I've made a number of bed frames and no one has given me an invitation!"

We had some colored-drinking glasses made from discarded bootleg liquor bottles. The treasured utensils were created by cutting off the tops with a circle of hot wire. From my art classes in grade school I showed crayon drawings on small pieces of treasured drawing paper. There were also boxes and folded furniture, part of plans for future rooms when things got back to normal. One pupil at the corner of his room had marked off a triangular space. When I asked him what it was, and he said that it was for a blanket to be hung to mark off his cubicle.

In addition, women painstakingly sewed and decorated garments from older clothing and stuffed toys from bits of clothes. Toys were also made from wood and bamboo. Cloth horses' heads attached to bamboo sticks for pretend horses were some I recollect. Some painted, while others made Japanese flower arrangements as taught by Nellie McKim. There were also wood carvings and chess pieces.

One of the toys never exhibited was a whistle. Soon after we moved to Camp Holmes, one of the older men offered to make toys for each of the children. His first suggestion was bamboo whistles. The women's committee threatened him with "death worse than hanging." The question they posed to him, "Can you imagine this camp filled with sixty or so kids blowing whistles night and day?" He beat a quick retreat, for the women's committee was something to be reckoned with by the male population of camp.

For the first Christmas at Camp Holmes, the women's committee and others made a toy for each child in camp to be delivered by a supposed Santa Claus, dressed in something red and his own beard. Carol received a beautiful fish that would stand out today in any stuffed toy exhibit. Its body, about 12 inches long and six inches wide, was made from scraps from an old evening gown in peach changeable taffeta covered with a heavy purple net for scales. Its fins were purple satin. I copied a pattern from an intact teddy brought into camp, and made a teddy bear for her out of an old, blue flannel blanket.

These outbursts of ingenuity also included the one wedding we had in camp. A missionary nurse and a miner had fallen in love. After families were finally permitted to live together in the barracks and the Baby House, they asked permission of the Japanese to marry. I guess the old adage "All the world loves a lover" was true of the Japanese as well, because they gave their permission.

All their friends loaned them wedding finery for the bride, bridesmaids and flower girls. An impressive ceremony with music followed. It was held in the grassy area where we held worship services. I could not attend as I was confined to the hospital with a severe case of jaundice, but they allowed me to come downstairs and sit on the porch so that I could at least have a glimpse of the joyous occasion.

Everyone who knew them gave gifts with great generosity. Jessie Junkin, a close friend, gave the bride an ancient, embroidered Chinese jacket that she had managed to bring into camp. Of course, there was criticism and discontent at this event, from those who had opposed families living together.

Chapter 25
...the desire to survive...

The "living together" of families caused more uproar and hostility than anything else that took place in camp among the internees. Close friendships were broken up and tempers flared. Accusations were made as to our being unpatriotic because the men fighting all over the world were separated from their families, and so to some it followed that we should not have that sense of security either. This was wartime and who were we to strive for normalcy? As I recall, Mr. Tomibe felt families should be together when "the turnover" came. Great was the upheaval after the votes were counted in favor of being united.

Everyone was affected as cubicles, formerly segregated according to sex, had to be moved, shelves torn down, and new assignments made to each of us. Space, so jealously guarded, had to be relinquished and new cubicles made and bunks relocated. This was all grudgingly accepted. Insults and sexual innuendo were bandied about by the opposing group. We missionaries came in for our share, as we had been unanimous about being reunited with our spouses. It was predicted that nine months from the day this obnoxious move was complete, babies would be arriving by the dozens. It did not come to pass as we pro-family parents had enough sense to know that pregnancies would be pretty stupid, considering our lack of food, energy, medical care, and the coming invasion of American forces. We simply wanted the protection of our husbands and the security of a reunited family unit. So the new took over from the old amid much hostility, hammering and the hanging of blankets around each new cubicle.

Change is always difficult, but with the stress of interment there was real cause for anger. Pent-up feelings from the past two years were focused on this one event. In retrospect, it is ironically hilarious, since getting families together is basically "the American way," but accusations of unpatriotic actions and sexual motivations for such a plan caused a real upheaval, emotionally and physically. Each side was equally self- righteous about "their cause." However, thanks to Mr. Tomibe's foresight and a camp committee, the change was made and we slowly settled into being civil again to each other.

I don't remember the exact arrangement in the Baby House, except for the front room that we were assigned to. Three couples with a baby each had a space about five feet wide by seven feet in depth. The most ingenious new cubicle for us "sex maniacs" was the Junkin's. Bill was the most inventive of people. We all hung the parents' double bunk from the ceiling. Bill cut a hole in the side of the house, where the bunk was to go, so that their bed extended outside under the generous eaves. Then he arranged a pulley system of ropes, which pulled the crib to the ceiling during the day time so that he, Jessie, and Billy had the whole floor space for their abode.

Our cubicle was next to theirs, and we were fortunate to have a window in which I hung sheer curtains sent from our house. Our bed, with a ladder hung from the ceiling, Carol's crib, a table, two canvas stools, and Carol's small chair with a tray filled our deluxe suite. Our table had been made by the shop from the wooden boxes in which the Red Cross supplies had been sent. The legs were made by removing every other post of the railing from the outside stairway of the barracks. We all treasured these tables as much as any highly polished mahogany table was ever cherished. The crib had been made from window screens Ed had "appropriated." There was also a screen to put on top of the crib to prevent mosquitoes from attacking. When we had friends in for the evening, I placed a cloth on top of the screened crib and used it as a serving table. Fortunately, Carol slept soundly and never rose up to send the cover crashing to the floor. We never had much to serve anyway, but it was a pure luxury to have a private spot all our own.

One of the outcomes of this move was truly amazing. Underneath the "topside" barracks was a crawl space. The inhabitants of the barracks above decided to shovel it out to make it deeper. They made low-ceilinged nooks into which they could crawl and have a more private spot than their cubicles above. To enter, you crouched through the tunnel-like area until you came to your cave-like abode. You immediately sat down upon improvised seating to avoid a "crick" in your back. They were like primitive cavemen but actually were highly educated teachers, engineers, miners and missionaries exalting in their ingenuity. The "caves" were decorated in "Camp Holmes period" stuff and made a snug nest for private conversation and entertaining. What a stark contrast for former Baguio residents whose homes had been spacious, comfortable, and at times even elegant.

This kind of transition wrought changes in our mind-set of what was really important in the overall scheme of things. One couple, who had been on the verge of a divorce even though they had lived at the country club in luxury, became reconciled in camp. The wife said to me once, "There, we had nothing and now we have each other." In the face of adversity and the loss of all their possessions, they were able to sift through emotions and feelings to find each other. Such dangerous and drastic changes should not be recommended by a marriage counselor, and of course, not all relationships fared that well. On the whole, common sense, courtesy, and the desire to survive helped us to maintain reasonably good relationships with our family and friends.

Chapter 26
...attitude...fashioned our stay

Trying to evaluate our internment, I suppose the word "attitude," fashioned our stay as "guests" of the Japanese Emperor. We were a small enough group that personal attitudes influenced the thinking of the group as a whole. Perhaps one of the most important was our ability to laugh at ourselves, or our captors' actions and their attitudes. One of the first examples of humor that I can recall was Marie Halsema sitting on her floor mattress in a queenly fashion, announcing to anyone nearby, "Well, this is just like Heaven! We all possess the same amount: nothing!"

Another example was that as the months passed, we began to realize how much the actions of one could influence the group as a whole. We were acutely aware of this and tried to conduct ourselves accordingly. I vividly remember Dana Nance's remark as we stood at the edge of the parade ground and watched as Clarence Mount received a brutal beating by the Japanese, collapsing into unconsciousness for "bootlegging" forbidden merchandise into camp, alcohol being one of the main items. Dana said, "All of us who used him should be there, too."

Another vividly remembered remark was made by Marge Patton to her 4 or 5 year old son, Bobby, when our camp was being torn up and abandoned for a trip to Manila and an unknown destination. Confusion, anger, and dismay reigned as we all hurriedly packed what we were allowed before boarding unmarked trucks that transported us to the lowlands. It was a frightening time, even for adults. Bobby remarked, "Now, we have no home!" Without hesitation Marge comforted him by saying, "Wherever Mommy and Daddy and you are, that is home." Today's kids need that same reassurance in poverty or wealth, and many do not have such comforting words.

Chapter 27
...monotony...pessimism and optimism

The days at Camp Holmes dragged by, month after month. I remember a moment of our next-to-the-last Christmas at Camp Holmes. Everyone worked on small gifts. The cooks reserved some of our food from Thanksgiving until Christmas so we were looking forward to as good a meal as could be conjured up from our meager selection of food. A few decorations graced the barren barracks and the Baby House, and on Christmas Eve all was ready. A pageant and reenactment of Christ's birth was performed as the audience sat on the hill below the barracks on a breathtaking, star-lit night. Ingenious costumes, baby goats, solemn children, young teen-age shepherds, three kings in richly colored robes, and a lovely Mary made us all forget the dreary and anxious times we were being forced to endure. Always at such times, the wonderful talent of our tiny community shone through, especially in the well-directed music and singing which comforted and gave us inward peace. Guards and guarded, again shared in a strange communion of hope and beauty. Inwardly, we were all sick of war. After the pageant ended, we quietly visited awhile with friends and drifted back to our bunks.

Before we knew it, it was early morning. Before sunrise, from outside the Baby House came the inspiring voices of skinny, shabby, and half-starved carolers. Carol and I were by the window. I awakened her, held her closely and told her Daddy was outside singing songs about the baby Jesus. There was still enough moonlight to reflect her beautiful brown eyes. She seemed to sense the moment of wonder, too. Even as they sang, the carolers were surrounded by guards and guns. Once or twice, I heard the click of guns as the guards tested the readiness of their arms.

I wonder what their thoughts were as they went about their rounds of Camp escorting the caroling group, which had gotten up before dawn to sing to their fellow prisoners. Perhaps they caught some of the spirituality of the moment. As I tucked Carol back into bed, thoughts of the uncertain future crowded my mind and I could only pray for her safety.

We received coveted news by the radio in the hospital as our forces moved, painstakingly slowly and at great loss of life, northward towards the Philippines. As food became scarcer, some died of various ills. Twelve in all, I believe, were buried on a hill above camp. Burial had to be done immediately, and if one was expected to die, some of the work crews would begin to build a coffin. One old timer in the hospital, who was thought to be in that condition, heard hammering one day outside of the hospital. Knowing why it was occurring, he reacted in anger. One of the lucky ones, he lived to be finally reunited with his Filipino family after our release.

As the months wore on, the lumber for coffins became more and more scarce. For one person they used a wooden, dining room table. One of the little girls asked her mother why they did that, and the not-so-comforting reply was, "Well, if we don't have food we don't need the tables."

Although censored and limited to a certain number of words, several times we were allowed to send mail via Red Cross. We all tried ingenious wording to convey our condition to those back home. Also, we received messages once or twice from parents and friends in the United States. One such message that Ed and I received was from a member on the mission board at the Annual Conference of the Church of the Brethren. He told us how all the former China missionaries got to together for a delicious Chinese dinner. As a hint, if you ever have friends in an internment camp, please refrain from telling them about food. Food was becoming of purer quality, but less quantity as the time passed, and we began hoarding for the coming turnover.

Toward the end of our stay at Camp Holmes, we saw some sparse air activity. One day an American plane flew

On to Manila!

over head and we all let out audible cheers. One of the
guards was nearby. He grinned and held up two fingers for
the "victory" sign and laughed. Boy, was that an attitude!
Later, we were warned by the Japanese not to react to
planes. As our forces came closer, our optimism waxed
and waned. Once, as we were expressing our fears,
impatience, and hopes of release, Don Zimmerman said

"Maybe they (our troops) spied on our camp and thought the guards and guarded had really 'lost it' and they'd just by-pass us."

Rumors abounded. One woman wondered how long it took for a rumor to get around camp, so she told a friend a wild one. It took 24 hours until it got back to her.

One true and really substantial rumor was that Leyte had fallen. Jim Halsema heard the rumor on his way to cook an egg at the hospital, and was so excited he tossed it in the air! Camp spirits were renewed as we occasionally saw American planes, except for one dreadful time when a plane flew low over camp with smoke trailing behind it. We later heard it had crashed above us in the mountains.

Thus, monotony ruled, with pessimism and optimism careening constantly through our thoughts. After orders came for the Baby House occupants to be moved topside, events moved rapidly. An early rumor after a slim Christmas proved only too true. We were to be moved to Manila. The things we had treasured, like shelves, bottles, tin cans, worn-out clothing, paper bits, and mattresses were all trashed as we frantically decided what to take and what to abandon. The state of our minds was reflected in the chaos of our usually neat camp. After the majority of internees were moved, a skeleton crew headed by Carl Eshbach stayed behind to "organize" the trash and return the camp to some semblance of order.

Chapter 28
...the terrible cost of war

We were only allowed a certain amount of baggage and were loaded into crowded, unmarked trucks with Japanese soldiers driving down Zig Zag Road. The way our driver drove made us believe he had imbibed one too many just to give him courage for the trip. Our trucks, not being marked with a Red Cross, were surely targets for our own Air Force. We had heard that there were daily bombings on the road, and there was a great deal of Japanese troop movement coming north as we headed south. In our truck, seated on the top of a large container of gasoline, was a Japanese soldier hovering over us with a gun and bayonet. I'm sure it was a bad time for him, too, as he had to guard this unhappy bunch of internees moving to the lowlands.

It was unbelievably crowded. The first "rest stop" we had was in a field which had been cleared on both sides of the road. As we alighted from the truck, the men dashed to one side of the road in order to have some privacy between the sexes. The guards ordered the men back, and we all had to relieve ourselves in full view of one another; however, by this time we didn't care.

The next stop was in a small town square. Filipinos gathered as we got off the truck. In the square hung a gallows, a grim reminder of the treatment that the Filipinos suffered constantly under Japanese occupation. This time, several blankets were held up by the women as we each took care of our needs. Carol refused to go because her potty was packed away, and she would not give in until we reached our destination and could unpack the potty.

On the way down, our truck had to make a stop as Japanese foot soldiers marched by. One of them reached up to the truck and handed Carol a banana. At that time bananas were selling for 50 pesos apiece, if available, and I'm sure it was quite a sacrifice for him. It was a wonderful moment of goodwill in a nasty, dangerous situation, and a wonderful treat for Carol.

As we rumbled on into the lowlands, hot, humid weather engulfed us, and the crowded truck became even more intolerable. Our destination, the notorious Bilibid Prison, loomed ahead of us, forbidding and frightening. It had been built by the Spaniards and used subsequently by Filipinos and Americans. High guard towers rose above us as we stopped at the formidable prison gate. Now we were to be in a real prison, condemned sometime ago and partially torn down. As it neared midnight, the iron gate slowly opened and our truck entered. Eerie does not even begin to describe the atmosphere as we wended our way through the paved streets, and past prison cells where men from Corregidor were kept since the infamous Death March. All of our hearts sank when we saw the squalid, horrid prison where so many had suffered throughout the years.

When we reached the center of the prison, another gate opened and we beheld our new home for the first time. With shattered spirits, we unloaded our few possessions. Others had arrived before us and warned us of the filth, bedbugs, and poor sanitary facilities. With limited supplies, they had tried to clean our new home, but days went by before there was any semblance of our usual orderliness and cleanliness. Actually, in the time spent there, battling bed bugs and dirt, the real battle for the city of Manila raged about us.

Bilibid Prison was an unbelievable dismal dwelling place in comparison to the spacious grounds and beautiful scenery of Camp Holmes in Trinidad Valley. The one consoling thought was that surely "the turnover" must be near. The stark ugliness of the partially torn down prison was overwhelming. Gray was the color that smothered the enclosed grounds and buildings. Grime and grit was the enemy of all of us.

Combined with the dirt and bed bugs, there were other "amenities" that contributed to our dreadful living conditions, such as the "crashing windows." The original windows had been removed and replaced with long pieces of galvanized iron, hinged at the top and propped open by a

rod braced on the sill. During the battle of Manila, when
nearby explosions occurred, these huge, narrow panels
closed with such terrific force and ear-splitting noise
against the building that we never knew whether we had
been hit or if it was just the usual concussion of iron
against cement.

Outside the main building was a row of open prison
cells. Bars were on the front and back. The only solid
walls were those dividing each cell. These cells were
immediately put to use as our "new" hospital. One cell was
reserved for an all purpose use. For several Sundays,
informal church services were held here until a Japanese
bomb exploded right outside the wall of the prison. This
bombing killed several United States soldiers, manning a
battery of mortars. After the arrival of our forces, each day
brought more sorrow and anxiety, as we got acquainted
with individual GIs. After visiting us, they would go out
into the deadly battle. The statistics of those injured and
killed were fifty percent.

The saddest spot of all in this melancholy setting was
the pathetic row of graves from former military prisoners.
Crude, wooden crosses had been erected on each grave by
their imprisoned comrades. Its desolate appearance
saddened us all, and brought more clearly to our hearts
and minds the terrible cost of war.

As our once well-ordered existence of Camp Holmes
became a memory, the committee again began to
heroically set goals to meet immediate needs. Thus, we
grudgingly hunkered down to the new challenge of "making
do" with less and less each day.

(We later learned that it was actually a fortunate move.
Baguio and the surrounding countryside ended up being
the last stand made by the Japanese. Their retreat
through the north resulted in surrender. The city of
Baguio was destroyed with saturation bombing.)

These were the starkest circumstances our camp had
ever faced. Each of us had to endure less living space, less
privacy, less food, along with a growing sense of the near
and dreaded but wished-for turnover.

The main building had two stories. Along with other
families we were given space upstairs. Fran and Father

Bartter of the Episcopal mission said that they would like to live next to us. They were an elderly couple with an unflagging sense of humor. We enjoyed getting to know them more intimately amidst the bed bugs, banging windows, kids, dirt, rumors, and horrible food. They entertained the children and Carol became their constant companion. Father Bartter fascinated the kids blowing smoke rings from his cigarettes. Fran, as she smoked, would tap her cigarette and say, "Another nail in my coffin!"

One incident which made her unhappy, involved Father Bartter and a rather small bath towel about his middle. He had to traipse from outdoors, up the stairs and to their space. Fran complained about the towel not meeting at his side, to which he calmly answered, "My dear, that is a V for Victory!"

Getting adequate food in a besieged city and the fear of city water mains being destroyed were our most immediate concerns. Due to the low calorie count, we moved listlessly throughout our everyday activities. Mr. Bergamini remarked that we looked like a movie in slow motion. Even the children became inactive. Sickness and malnutrition over took many, and the inadequate, outdoor hospital quickly became full. Medicine was in short supply and carefully doled out to those who were the most ill.

By now, our food consisted of poor quality rice and corn meal, roughly ground and heavily endowed with weevils. After being strained, gritty, dry soy bean residue was sent to us from a nearby hospital. Hopefully, the dry residue contained some nutrition. On several occasions, if the guards had had their rice for the day, they would carefully lay their extra rice in the garbage and allow only the children to come and scoop out handfuls of the leftovers. I'm not at all sure it was "leftovers," for they were scrounging for their food, too. As they stood nearby watching the children get their "extras," they were satisfied.

A short time after our arrival, the air attacks increased. The constant roar of the planes was deafening. Constant tension filled each of us as we tended to daily needs. Constant fear of the coming turnover filled our minds, but somehow life continued. We endured, and hope became our constant companion, softening the harsh reality of our nightmarish reality.

We knew that soldiers from Corregidor and the Death March were next door. They had been spotted as several groups from Baguio had arrived in the course of three or four days, but no contact with them was allowed by the Japanese. Our choir decided to try to communicate to these men by standing close by the rough, gray wall and

Being Shelled!

124

singing hymns and familiar songs, hoping that these military prisoners would hear us, know we were aware of their presence, and that we were trying to connect with them in some small way.

Upon moving into Bilibid, writings from former U.S. prisoners were found on some of the walls, which with vivid, heartbreaking language expressed their strong feelings about their Japanese captors and reflected their terrible treatment. Their endurance had been tried to the breaking point, expressed in the written expression of their suffering under unnecessarily cruel, harsh treatment. The writing was for some their last, desperate effort to tell the outside post-war world what they had endured. Some of our men made it their duty to copy down these writings to be turned over later to the proper authorities.

A happening of miracle proportions occurred on the trip from Baguio to Bilibid. During the move, which took three or four days, we had been so fearful of being transferred in unmarked trucks, but for those four days there was no bombing on the road. We naively thought that "our American forces knew we were being moved, and therefore restrained from bombing during those particular days." Later, some aviators who had been on the aircraft carrier, explained that during that time they were short a fuel shipment from the States and were simply unable to do any bombing.

Upon hearing this coincidence most of us believed that God's hand was in this. This is one subject that is very troubling to me. When we arrived home, upon visiting churches, they all said, "Our prayers were with you and so you were saved." But prayers were with those who lost their lives. Why would not God protect them too? Troubling theology, but all through this experience there were unexplained periods when things were hopeless and dangerous and we lived. Survivors of great tragedies the world over have these same feelings, but how humbling it all is.

Our section of Bilibid had minimal sanitary conditions. All of the plumbing had been ripped out prior to the war as the old prison was in the starting phases of demolition. The former Army prisoners, who had lived in that section of Bilibid, erected a crude, toilet facility which consisted of a slanted wooden trough. At the high end was a bucket on a hinge of sorts with water dripping into it. As the bucket filled, it tipped over, washing the contents of the trough into a sewer opening. To use this contraption, one had to straddle the trough in a very undignified manner to relieve oneself. Four or five people could use it at one time.

For the first few days this was uncovered except on the sides where woven mats had been placed upright for some sense of dignity. Humiliating as it was, we had no choice but to use it. Fortunately, some green mosquito netting was found and our men covered our amazing privy. The Japanese reacted immediately, ordering it to be taken down as the netting belonged to the Japanese Imperial Army and by using it we were insulting the Emperor. It was carefully, but firmly, explained that the waste had to be shielded or flies and dysentery would overwhelm our camp. The netting stayed.

There were also crude, open showers. We had to use them each day as the dust and dirt from destruction of buildings and fighting swirled about us. These were also surrounded by flimsy, woven reed mats but uncovered at the top. The men were discouraged from looking out the upstairs lobby windows, for it was also a good place to gaze down upon the showers. We were a skinny, emaciated bunch of women, but even so, several women always kept watch to make sure that no wandering male eyes gazed upon us, while checking on the on-going destruction of the city The city was as sad a sight as we women had become.

As always, obtaining food was an immediate concern to us and our guards. Each day we had to scrounge for our food, competing with others in a city now doomed to be destroyed, ravaged, and set afire. The committee divided us into groups of fifteen with one internee in each group responsible for getting communications from the committee to us.

Ed was head of our group. One day he received a notice from the committee to read to us. He remembers the note as follows: "Due to the unauthorized efforts of a member of the Japanese staff, we have received an extra ration of rice, bringing our total ration to 600 grams per day. Please destroy this notice as soon as you have read it to your group." It was destroyed so that that particular guard would not get into trouble. Any increase in food at that time was a small miracle of sorts, and that it was supplied under great duress by a single Japanese again spoke of man's humanity to man.

During this lull before the Americans arrived, one of the Japanese guards brought Carol a small rag doll. Such gestures were touching beyond words as we each, guards and prisoners alike, knew that our armies would soon be locked in deadly battle. As our planes daily flew overhead and rumors grew of the coming Americans, our committee told our guards that if they stayed with us, we would guarantee their safety because of their care for us. When the fighting began, the guards left, saying they belonged to the Emperor and must go out and meet their destiny. There was both joy and sorrow when this event took place.

Each day planes flew out high over Manila sometimes in formation and sometimes singly. Cheers and hope would erupt simultaneously until one day an anti-aircraft gun hit its target. The plane burst into flames as the parachutes ejected with the two men, but tragically the parachutes caught fire too, and the doomed men fell to their deaths. This hushed the cheers of all of us and feelings ran deep in grief. It was especially hard on the children as the glory of the daily flights crashed in cruel reality among us. The next day a touching ceremony took place. A formation of planes flew overhead with one empty space representing the lost plane as they dropped a wreath in memory of their fallen comrades.

Chapter 29
...there was a bond and respect between us...

The arrival of the Americans in Manila began on
February 3, 1945. Strange vehicles called "jeeps" rolled by
our prison on their way to Santo Tomas University to
release the five thousand civilian prisoners held there.
They were unaware of the presence of "Bataan Death
March" prisoners in Bilibid. They thought our group was
still in Baguio and that the Corregidor survivors had been
removed. MacArthur had sent these troops hurriedly to
north Manila to free Santo Tomas, and they had rushed
south for three days after their landing to the north. Our
Japanese guards had gone up on the roof of our building
and threw crude hand grenades as our troops passed. The
Americans had thought Bilibid was solely occupied by
Japanese.

One report had it that one American captain, noticing a
small wooden door at the side of the prison wall, had
shouted, "Surrender!" The answer came back in English,
"Hell, we can't surrender! We're Americans!" With that
startling news, the Americans withdrew until plans could
be made to safely enter the prison.

The next day Carl Eshbach called us all to the
downstairs lobby area. As we all stood there crowded
together, the Japanese guards came down from the rooftop
loaded with hand grenades. Then nervously, but calmly,
they walked out the open gate to meet their destiny, just as
they had previously said they would. They knew what it
would be like as American tanks surrounded our prison.
As they left, one little boy ran up and took the hand of a
Japanese soldier with whom he had played and started to
walk out with him. His mother had to pull him back from
the retreating Japanese and the open door. As the
Japanese passed through our crowded meeting place, they
could have easily thrown the grenades at us in one last
defiant act but because of the past days at Bilibid spent

together, there was a bond and respect between us, earned by both sides as we strove together for survival.

The reason for Carl calling us together was to read the amazingly-worded document that the Japanese had given him a few moments before. It read as follows:

1.   The Japanese Army is now going to release all prisoners of war and internees here on our own accord.
2.   We are assigned to another duty and shall be here no longer.
3.   You are at liberty to act and live as free persons, but you must be aware of probable danger if you get out.
4.   We shall leave here food stuffs, medicine and other necessities of which you may avail yourself for the time being.
5.   We have arranged to put up a sign board at the front gate having the following context: "Lawfully released prisoners of war and internees are quartered here. Please do not molest them unless they make positive resistance."

When the Japanese took a hasty departure and Carl had read our "official release," cheers and tears ruled the moment. At that point, someone remembered the American flag the women had sewn surreptitiously during the days at Camp Holmes. This was victoriously brought out and hung on the top of the building. Immediately, the Japanese began firing at our home-made Star Spangled Banner. It was hastily withdrawn.

Believe me, we made no "positive resistance" to our American forces as they triumphantly entered our prison the next day. Hugs, cheers, and tears were the order of the day as we uproariously welcomed these men, so far from home, so long fighting, and so longing to see the war end.

After our guards left and we were left to await the arrival of the Americans, it was a very iffy situation. That afternoon Ed hung some newly laundered clothes on a line outside the main building. Immediately, a Japanese flame thrower came in and hit the clothes directly, burning them up completely. I always wished that I had saved the charred clothing, but at that time souvenir saving was not the first priority on our minds.

The night before, as the Americans had surrounded the prison with tanks, those of us on the upper floor of Bilibid were ordered to the safety of the downstairs. Friends clustered together, greedily opening supplies of food we had saved for just such a moment. With the wonderful knowledge of the arrival of our troops, the most primitive satisfaction surfaced, gorging ourselves on food without worrying about the future supply. That joy may have been short lived if the battle had somehow gone in favor of the Japanese, but our confidence overwhelmed all such thoughts and misgivings. The eerie night passed in excitement, and the feeling of unreality that the "turnover" had finally come about. And, so far, we had survived.

The next day we overwhelmed the Americans with enthusiastic greetings and hugs as they entered our section of the prison. In spite of being in combat, they were healthy and sturdy men. They patiently endured the enthusiasm and questions. One question I remember someone asking was who the Vice President was, to which the officer answered, "Some guy named Truman!"

Though weary from three days of fighting their way from Lingayan Gulf to Manila, they eagerly shared with us news and a comradeship that nourished us spiritually far beyond the food that they so lavishly brought to us. Their part in releasing fellow Americans, skinny and poorly clothed as we were, made them feel some satisfaction for the terrible suffering that they had endured during the three long years of war in the South Pacific. Especially welcoming to them were the children. The kids followed them around constantly, and they in turn patiently endured the elated children. Often they would bring us jeeps and ride round and round the narrow camp yard with the kids piled in, yelling in their new freedom and joy.

Each day with heavy shelling overhead and fighting all about us, these weary men would came looking for internees from their home state. They brought extra treats of food that they thought we would enjoy. In addition, the Army supplied us with such a voluminous supply of food, that after three years of bare subsistence, we were stunned at such unbelievable plenty. The GIs hated the Army rations, but to us it seemed almost like gourmet food. Most of us had small charcoal stoves made from five gallon tin cans. On these we took the C rations and concocted recipes with ingredients beyond our wildest "Camp" dreams. The most popular was the fudge we made and shared with the GIs.

Santo Tomas had not fared as well as we did in the turnover. When our troops approached, there were skirmishes, death and injuries as the Americans internees were freed. As our camp was smaller in number, we were also in better health and spirits. In fact, ten times smaller as they numbered 5,000 and we were only 500. Until we were "dumped" into Bilibid, we had also had a better climate, being high in the mountains where the average temperature was 70 degrees. In addition, we had higher caliber people: educated, cooperative in forming a community, and seeing the value of working together for the good of all. Even the military commented on the contrast. From the tales we had heard of Santo Tomas, each group there acted and thought as a separate, competing, conflicting group. We had acted similarly at first, but as we quickly became acquainted, we realized that if we didn't "all hang together, we'd hang separately." Add to that the hot humid weather of the lowlands, and their condition physically and mentally was much worse than ours.

During this time of the turnover, there was daily bombing and shelling overhead. It was reported that Manila had the heaviest shelling of WWII except for Warsaw, Poland. It was estimated that it would take forty years to rebuild the ravaged, destroyed city. The dust and debris swirling around this former beautiful city from daily bombings, and hand-to-hand street fighting covered everything, including us. The stench from the dead or dying permeated the city. It was a sick, sweet smell, never to be forgotten. Each day, reports came in of government buildings alternatively occupied by the Japanese and Americans. In a matter of just three weeks, the city was totally destroyed.

131

Chapter 30
...the generous meaning of democracy

Several days after our release, huge flames approached our prison as fire swept uncontrollably through the city. In desperation, the Japanese had set Manila afire. Having heard an untrue rumor that Bilibid had been mined, within a short period of time, tired, weary troops came to rescue us in trucks and jeeps. They loaded the women and children as quickly as possible and the men started to walk, both groups carrying the few possessions that they allowed us to take.

Once again, we had to leave behind some of the few possessions we had brought from Baguio. The high, wild, uncontrollable flames were now only two blocks away. They also had to care for the pitiful Corregidor prisoners, quickly loading them and rushing north to Ang Tibay, a shoe factory thought to be out of the range of the Japanese fire. Some of these men, confused and terrified by three years of prison, fought off the Americans even as they tried to rescue them. Many were so malnourished that even with food, they died.

As we stood and waited our turn to get into the rescue vehicles, several of the British women hung back. The GIs, rather impatiently motioned for them to climb into the trucks. They answered, "But we're British!" The GIs replied, "You're prisoners. It makes no difference to us. Get in the trucks!" With this, several of them broke down and cried, finally realizing the generous meaning of democracy. (At the time the American Red Cross supplies had arrived in Camp Holmes, the British were surprised that we all shared, regardless of nationality. They had thought that only Americans would benefit from American supplies.) As they boarded the trucks, they said that if these were British troops, the British would have been loaded first.

Our escape from the encroaching fire was filled with drama and tension. As the trucks and jeeps finally pulled away from Bilibid, we were surrounded on each side by men of the 37th Infantry. They and the 1st Cavalry had been the ones to rush to the northern part of Manila, where we Americans had been held captive. Carol and I were placed in a jeep. There was a driver and one other officer accompanying us. This officer immediately took off his helmet and placed in on Carol's head to protect her from any gunfire, as we were in an actual battle zone. In doing this, he was putting himself in great danger. He manned a machine gun, which he kept rotating back and forth in case of enemy fire.

In the meantime, the men in our camp were told to walk towards the Ang Tibay shoe factory on the outskirts of the city. We were all a bit apprehensive about this because the city was not only on fire, but was also a battleground.

As the men walked, they were greeted by Filipinos who cheered them on as they passed by. The men were overwhelmed by this. One man in particular was so touched that he impetuously gave the beautifully embroidered table linens that he was carrying for his wife to the Filipino woman who had given him such welcomed water. She was a lucky woman, but he was one unlucky man when his wife later found out what had happened to the one treasured possession that she had saved for all those years. Fortunately, for all of us, the men were soon picked up by newly arrived volunteers in trucks, and they, too, arrived safely at Ang Tibay.

We shall always hold in esteem those brave men who volunteered to come rescue their fellow Americans. They had had days of hard fighting without rest, and, yet with rest available to them, they put their lives on the line to come save us.

A glow from the fire, only two blocks away, cast a surreal aura over the entire desperate scene. The Ang Tibay factory was next to a brewery, where the Army had located before coming to our rescue. When they first arrived, they had the welcome diversion of filling their helmets with beer, pouring it over their heads, and gulping the welcome brew to refresh themselves after a non-stop drive into the city. MacArthur ordered this drive to get to the American prisoners before harm came to us by the trapped Japanese.

When we arrived, they put us on the second floor balcony overlooking the downstairs factory. There they placed the prisoners who had been on the other side of our walls at Bilibid. Finally, we were face-to-face with these men, and face-to-face with the ravages their bodies and minds had suffered during three years of sheer hell. It was truly a horrible sight. These men were in pitiable conditions. Some were on stretchers; others were barely able to move. They had been in such abject health that when their fellow prisoners had been shipped to Japan on the "Hell ships," the Japanese had left them behind because of their deplorable health situation. It was a scene that would be seared into our consciousness forever.

It has always been difficult to explain the difference in their treatment and ours in Baguio at the hands of the Japanese Imperial Army. I think the thought is that, first of all, we were civilians. Secondly, we had small children in our camp. The Japanese are known for their indulgence of young children. Thirdly, we had a fairly cohesive group who worked through our camp leaders, especially Nellie McKim, who knew the Japanese culture and all the delicate nuances necessary to communicate effectively.

Also, we were a relatively small group, and both the guards and guarded, were isolated in the mountains, separated from constant contact with the guards' higher officers. The Japanese at our camp were given this duty of guarding 500 Americans as sort of a rest and recreation time, although at times they must have been thoroughly sick of us as we certainly were of them. But some of the constantly abhorrent treatment in most camps, particularly military, was for the most part only occasionally present in our camp. There was fear, uncertainty, and constant food shortages, but not terror every waking moment as some camps experienced.

As this array of prisoners was being tenderly placed below us, there was a hastily set-up broadcasting station of sorts. The announcer was triumphantly telling the people in the United States that Manila had fallen. It was ours and all was under control. Because of that, any war bulletin I have heard since, I have taken with a "large grain of salt." Manila did not fall until several weeks later.

We stayed at the factory overnight, were given cots, and set about to adapting to a new place. By this time, such changes were just a part of life, but this was particularly exciting as for the first time in a long time we felt safe and secure.

However, the next morning after a more-than-hearty breakfast, the Japanese had moved into our range and they began shelling the area. The officers decided that Bilibid was a safer place for us because of the high, thick walls. The fire was over and Bilibid was untouched, so we were loaded back into jeeps and trucks for a return ride to our late abode in Manila.

Ed accompanied us this time. We made a quick dash from Ang Tibay to Bilibid. Gun fire could be heard in the distance, but we felt secure in our Army escort. I'm not so sure they did, but once more they risked their lives to take us to safety. Bilibid had been searched for mines for there had been a rumor that the Japanese had mined it before their departure. So, still living on rumors and counter rumors, we made our way back "home."

On the way, one of the GIs in our vehicle gave Carol a pack of fruit-flavored Life Savers. Never having seen packaged candy, she cautiously opened the package, glanced at it, and then slowly closed it. I asked her, "How come you didn't take one? That is good candy." She nonchalantly replied, "Well, it's broken!" Here was this refugee kid spurning the Life Savers because they had holes in the middle. Within three weeks she had developed an elitist discernment. We finally convinced her it was all right to eat candy with holes in it. The poor GI must have thought we had a truly strange child on our hands.

When we arrived back at Bilibid, we were shocked to find that the prison had been looted and ran-sacked. Anything of value had been taken by the Filipinos. Their impression had been that we were leaving for good, so they felt free to help themselves. Our troops were too busy fighting the Japanese or fires to stand guard at an empty prison. So once more our possessions were reduced, we now had only the few things we had been allowed to take to Ang Tibay the night of the fire.

However, we were still alive and relatively safe. Not so for some other Americans and Filipinos south of the Passig River. They had been herded into a church building, which had been set afire and they all had burned to death. News of such suffering abounded as the battle for Manila proceeded. The Filipinos suffered unspeakable horrors for they had no way of escape and were trapped in a city under siege.

The Japanese made their last stand in the ancient, walled city that the Spanish had built centuries before. Certainly these walls could have told amazing tales as the centuries and the history of Manila unfolded. The Japanese had been holed up in there for days and the Americans were desperate to gain control.

Ed and I were privileged to have had a bit of insight and anticipation of the final collapse of Japanese resistance. Mary and Bob Dyer at Bilibid lived nearby, and they shared this experience with us. An officer, who was a friend of Mary's back home, looked them up invited them to officer headquarters for dinner. Actually, Mary was asked to "sing for her dinner" since she had a beautiful voice. They had a wonderful experience, "topped off" with "top secret" information. As they visited, they heard the military plans for the next day pertaining to the overthrow of the walled city. The officers talked over their plans as follows: At a certain time the Navy was to come up the river and shell the walled city. At the same time, the Air Force would bomb it, and the ground forces would surge in to finish the battle. This was to start at 10:00 a.m. Sure enough the assault began as we heard planes over head and shelling from the river exactly on time. It was an eerie, strange feeling to anticipate these actions and to then hear them actually happening.

On our return to Bilibid, we went through the dirt and rubble trying to once again make the place livable. On doing so, I found a small, red, lacquer bowl we had bought at an ancient lacquer factory in our "hutung" or alley where the language school was located. Also found were three pieces of Cloisonne salt and pepper shakers that we had purchased. One salt dish was never found. The other object that I regretted losing from Peking was a set of brass bookends, on which were set old carvings from the roof of a torn down temple. These were the only things left from our prewar existence and now they were gone. But we still had each other and, hopefully, a future.

During the days of the battle for Manila and all the three years of our internment, there was a terrible, murderous war being fought. The loss of life and the post war suffering from its effects can never be totaled or imagined. During the fighting in Manila, our casualties were fifty percent. These are just numbers of our forces. Filipino civilians and others in the city were not counted. That we survived and lived to have a future is one of life's mysteries. Even as we reveled in our release, enjoying the simple luxury of having food, new clothing, and hew hope, thousands were dead or dying outside the walls of Bilibid.

Chapter 31
It must not happen again...

Life took up a new rhythm of bare existence after the dirt and filth of the ransacked prison had been cleaned and sprayed thoroughly with the new DDT disinfectant. The Army assured us all germs would be gone. The spraying included us! Now thoroughly disinfected according to Army standards, life limped along amidst rumors and conjectures of what was to happen to us.

One welcome interlude occurred when an old acquaintance of the Junkins looked them up. He was from an LST, anchored in Manila Harbor, and he suggested that the Junkins invite some of their friends to come to his ship for dinner. So the next day the Junkins, Jack and Lucy Vinson, Don and Ruth Zimmerman, and Ed and I started out for our first adventure in freedom in three years. We left Carol with the Flory's and the Cunningham's as we felt it was too risky to take her along, since sporadic fighting still existed.

As I look back on it now, it wasn't the smartest thing to do. We walked down to the harbor, which was crowded with all kinds of Navy ships and personnel. As we waited for the landing barge to sweep ashore and miraculously open its doors, we talked with the sailors and inspected the small boats, all part of this great array of battle equipment which had made its way to the Bay of Manila. Not since Dewey, had that bay been inundated with so much battle gear, this time to defeat the Japanese. There still remained the half sunken ships, some with Japanese sailors still aboard. At night they tried to shell our vessels, but with little effect.

When the landing barge arrived, it had sailors aboard who were anxious to get on dry land and explore the ravaged city of Manila. We were excited to board it for the trip back to the LST. It took us right into the cavernous hold of the ship which overcame us with its vast empty space, which was as large as a football field. On the upper deck we received a warm welcome from the Navy and Jessie's friend.

First, they showed us where the restrooms were. We entered it with awe and a certain reverence for from the hot water faucets gushed hot water! We immediately fell to washing dusty faces, hands, arms, and legs. The joy of clean, hot water on a washcloth can be sheer ecstasy. We repeated this several times. Meanwhile, Billy kept flushing the toilet—a new toy for him--all the time inquiring if this were "home." We stayed in that glorious room for twenty or thirty minutes congratulating ourselves on our good fortune. We finally abandoned our adulation and left that glorious room. I'm sure the Navy guys were wondering what was taking so long.

We were then shown around the ship, and seated at a table with white linen, china and silverware. The waiters served us in truly regal, formal fashion. It was "regal" to us certainly for a well-set table was but a dim memory. All too soon, it was time to depart and go back to the reality daily combat, dust and odors, as the city still faced more destruction and death.

As we passed by the destroyed buildings, their layered, broken floors hung precariously downwards like leaves in an abandoned book. Jessie, Lucy, and I got ahead of the men and before long some Army men came along in a jeep and offered us a ride back to Bilibid. We accepted and without a scruple waved goodbye to our astonished husbands! When they let us out at the gate of Bilibid, three shots rang out. We looked at each other with some consternation, thinking of our husbands. At that low point, the American guard at our gate berated us for being out in the city while fighting was still going on. "You don't even have helmets on!" he said. Even we cannot go anywhere without helmets!" Being thoroughly chastised, we waited anxiously for our husbands to appear. They finally did, fortunately only making a few smart remarks about our being picked up.

In spite of being in dismal, gray Bilibid, the high walls gave a comforting sense of security. As we passed through the front area taken over by Army officers, I noticed a group of them around a desk. The young GI who was taking us back to the civilian area said that the tall, dark complexioned man was an American Indian. After living on the Navajo Reservation, I have often wondered if he was one of the famous Code Talkers. In Window Rock, in the early seventies, our Plateau Science Society gave a party for the Navajo Code Talkers on their return from Washington D.C, where they had finally been honored. In the South Pacific, these Navajos had used the complicated tonal Navajo language as a code to confuse the Japanese. Of course, it never was "broken." It wasn't until long after the war that this was finally revealed and the Navajos suitably honored.

After our release by the Japanese, the GIs, Air Force and Navy personnel visited Bilibid to look up friends or to meet those from their home state after years of fighting in the South Pacific. Several days after our release, General MacArthur visited, corncob pipe and all. He had personal friends in camp. Even though it was a battle zone, he did not wear a helmet. It's a fortunate thing he did not encounter the GI who scolded us for not having a helmet. He walked through the prison escorted by Carl Eschbach. He showed a sense of satisfaction that his hurried thrust into Manila had saved us. For us, he had finally "returned." If others in the military had had their way, the Philippine invasion would have come much later, if at all. Certainly our survival would have been in doubt. But in true "MacArthur style," he had promised "to return" and would not be persuaded otherwise. We were very fortunate. A few more months on that meager diet would have sealed the fate of many.

His visit and tour of our camp has another poignant side to it, experienced by Ruth Eschbach. She had returned home before the war because of her son's encroaching blindness. It was a Sunday night, in Cleveland, Ohio. She had spoken to a group of church young people in a wealthy area. She felt no response from them as she spoke of the war and was more than aware of their indifferent attitude. Alone and half sick at heart, she knew the Philippines had been invaded and the battle of Manila was in progress. She had no idea where Carl was.

140

She went to a theater and decided to relax and see a show. At this time, movies showed the current news as a prelude to the movie. As she sat there, the news of Manila's battle was flashed on the screen. A scene with Carl and MacArthur walking in Bilibid prison came on the screen. Stunned and relieved that Carl was alive, she sat there moved beyond words for the second showing. One can only imagine her feelings. Surely she was led there at that particular time to see that show.

Some days later, Jean MacArthur visited our ransacked prison abode. In gray, ancient, dusty old Bilibid, she appeared in a spotless, white silk dress with shiny, red shoes and purse, looking "voguish," seemingly untouched by the events swirling about her. She met with old friends, who were clad in ragged clothing, thin, weary and war worn. They felt resentment at her cheerful, benevolent greetings and appearance, and later groused about it as only prisoners can. We were all on edge from weeks of shelling and bombardment, from the evacuation, and from the return to the filthy, looted prison. I'm sure she had no idea how she appeared to us: an almost ghostlike form from a distant past. Simpler attire could have saved the day and the resentment.

One day a photographer came into Bilibid and gathered the smallest children together for a picture to be sent to the United States. As he hastily got the children together, I suggested that instead of just photographing the children each mother should hold her own child so that stateside families could recognize whose child was whose. He was extremely cross at this suggestion, but the mothers realized the point and each got in the picture holding their own child. When this picture was published in the United States, many families recognized the mother and thus identified the child. It was the first picture many grandparents saw of their young grandchildren. The picture was later published in the 1946 Yearbook Britannica under "child welfare" of all things.

Another foray to the "outside" of the destroyed city happened when a group of us attended a nearby church, which had escaped the savage battle. GIs, Filipinos and freed Americans were altogether. It was a solemn but joyous worship service. The minister spoke of new beginnings. The one dramatic sight for me was when the armed soldiers came in and stashed their guns on the rear pew of the church out of respect for being in a house of worship. It would be a more joyous occasion if fifty years later we had learned to stash weapons out of respect for human life in this so beautifully created world.

With the stench of death about us, we wondered what had happened to the Japanese guards who had so quietly left our camp futilely clutching hand grenades, which they could have so easily used in that crowded lobby after Carl had read our release. I thought of the one who had presented Carol with a small, rag doll, of the ones who scrounged around outside Bilibid for extra bits of food at their own peril, of the guard whose friendship had caused a little five-year-old Caucasian boy to clutch his hand as they neared the gate to follow them to the outside. I thought of the dead Japanese soldier left lying in the street, within sight of our upstairs window. After he had been killed, a Filipino stopped and removed his boots. As he left, he saluted the dead soldier. We thought of Mr. Tomibe, all his kindnesses, and wondered what may have happened to him. Some rumors said that all of our guards had died, while others claimed that some had escaped. In a sense we did not want to know. It was all very painful. Our camp was only a blip on the screen of a world gone mad with war. To multiply that by the thousands involved was all too much for a mind to grasp. Our one thought was that it must not happen again...

One hopeful event took place when Ed, Joe Smith, and others were asked to join some Filipino Christians to assess the future and direction of the Filipino church. The conclusion reached was that emphasis on denominations would cease, being that the war had united everyone. In addition, the Filipinos were to be in control of their own churches. To some extent this has been realized. For most mainline denominations, we now wait until the local churches request our assistance. After we had been home for about a year, Don Zimmerman said the churches in America must now turn to the former mission churches for new ideas and guidance, as they had grown and matured in ways we had yet to learn.

One evening after the fighting in Manila had ceased, we were all awaiting the news of how and when we were to go home when a young aviator visited Bilibid and met some of the girls in camp. A group of us were up on the roof of Bilibid where just a short time ago our guards had stood, throwing hand grenades at troops from the American Army. A few city lights were on in the distance, something we had not seen since our arrival, a soft breeze was blowing, and we were all relaxing in the strange quiet of no-battle noises. This aviator came and sat down with us. He told us he was being sent home because of battle fatigue. He seemed to need to talk, and we were all transfixed when he revealed that he had just returned from a bombing mission in Baguio. All of us there had friends and relatives in that area. He related how the Air Force had done saturation bombing. (Saturation bombing is planes flying in formation in one direction, bombing everything in their path. Another group then comes in at right angles and also bombs. Criss-crossing a city in this manner meant that total destruction of a city would take place.) Thus the lovely city of Baguio was destroyed. The Japanese had made their last stand there. A lovely town was leveled with heavy casualties to its inhabitants.

Later, we found out the Union Church, where Carl was pastor and most of the missionary group had attended, was gone. Fortunately, in constructing the floor of the church, the builder had miscalculated the amount of cement used for the floor. He had used double the amount needed. Filipino members, thinking American would not bomb churches, had gathered in the basement, so when they did bomb it, the thick cement floor withstood the bombing, and saved those huddled in the basement. Later it was used as a refuge for some of those whose homes had been destroyed.

The Notre Dame hospital where Carol was born was destroyed. In its rubble they found Mr. Halsema, Betty and Jim's dad. He was one of the men whose early work as an engineer in the Philippines only served to benefit the

Filipinos. He had also been the former mayor of Baguio where he had served them well. His unselfish labors in an emerging country can only be praised in the highest terms. After the war he was honored by the city, and one of the roads that he had engineered was named after him.

The reasoning behind bombing hospitals and churches was that the Americans had been told that the Japanese had stored munitions in them. This proved untrue, and many lives were lost that day. Betty's mother escaped as she did not go to the hospital. She, too, had taken her place in the developing of the Philippines. Of course, none of this was known to us as the obviously upset aviator related his story. Still we sat silently, only able to wonder what had happened to friends and relatives still in the Baguio area. Camp Holmes was also destroyed, and so we at Bilibid, finally realized how fortunate we had been.

Following are copies of letters Jim Halsema wrote to family and friends after a precarious trip to Baguio in the month of May, following our release on February 4, 1945.

Letter from Jim Halsema, April 15 (1945)

Manalo signed death certificate giving the cause of Pop's death as "Fatal injuries received from bomb fragments". The next day I wrote out a story of AP which was passed by censor after some argument and which you may already have seen.

Manalo said remaining Americans in Baguio gathered at Notre Dame Hospital in mid March owing to the danger from bombing and Japanese occupation of their homes. On the morning of March 15 bombers came over earlier than usual. Most people, including mother, went to the air-raid shelter but Pops preferred the toilet behind Manalo's office with concrete walls. Manalo stayed out doors. Several bombs hit the building. When survivors returned they found Pops' body buried under the concrete wall. Also killed were Mrs. Rogers and Mike Ryan. They were all buried near the grotto at the back of the hospital that same day. Mrs. Manalo said mother took it bravely and joined the others who went to the Catholic Church. She was not hurt in any war. When that was bombed she joined several others, including the Staffords and Muzzie Whitmarsh, and went to Chief Keith's house where there was an excellent shelter. The Manalos left the next day. Getting through the lines was risky exhausting business.

I felt relieved in a way to know positively what happened, but how to get mother to safety? Jim Hutchenson, AP correspondent, said North Luzon fighting, concentrated near Baguio and Balete Pass, will probably prove to be the hardest, longest and perhaps costliest of any battle in the Philippines. Japs are using artillery effectively because of good observation posts on mountain tops, but Yanks are countering with heavier artillery and bombings. Even so the Japs always bomb from shell and bombproof caves when the doughboys advance. It's a 24 hour a day war. Manalo says the Japs have tunneled through many hills, such as the one behind Home Sweet Home, but Mother is resourceful and she has many friends. I hope I can see her one of these days. She will require rest I'm sure before she can go back to the USA.

Cordy Job has a job with the Red Cross that has permanent possibilities. Gibby tutors MacArthur's son. Edna Miller works in Santo Tomas office. Del checks early morning kitchen workers. Ken Jorgensen is checking lumber resources in this part of the Luzon for the Army and Roxy is a secretary for some officer.

The food situation looks ok for the future. Peachy (Mrs. Whitmarsh's granddaughter) had me for lunch yesterday and served an omelet made from GI rations, powdered eggs and all, tasted like the fresh. She's working with the quartermaster officer to evolve recipes suitable for small scale use of Army food.

Manila, May 3, 1945

Dear Halsemas and Foleys,

Reporting on my Baguio trip.

The morning of April 30, Capt. Dahlstrom paged me over the Santo Tomas PA and told me to be ready at 9 am for a trip to Baguio. A 37th division MP who had just taken Max Schwaeble and two other Germans to Bilibid was returning northward. George Bell and Montenucci went along. We pushed along in the jeep along highway 3, obeying the 25 miles speed limit most of the time. Everywhere road gangs were repairing holes, graders were widening the road out to 30 feet when possible, and bridges were being repaired or rebuilt. At Tarlac we had doughnuts and coffee at a Red Cross canteen and I drove thenceforth. I noticed the greatest change in the San Fabian-Demortis area, where invasion beach heads have altered the countryside almost beyond recognition. A once narrow, winding country road is now a 3-lane boulevard. And further north work was going on to widen the old highway for heavy vehicles. We got to Bauag by 4:40 pm. George and the salesman took off for Baguio immediately --I had to confer with a fellow who wasn't there. Two somewhat inebriated truckers drove me up the Naguilian road at passenger car speed. This was a battleground of recent vintage. Naguilian was burned--the river spanned by a Bailey bridge. At frequent intervals neatly cleared spots showed where camps had been pitched by our troops. Telephone poles were festooned with field telephone wires. The village of Burgos was 100% erased from the map. Skeletons of burned-out Jap trucks lined the roadsides. Every few yards were caves scooped into the banks in which Japs tried to halt our progress. Sometimes they blew down the roads. But the mighty bulldozer conquered all. Squat, flat-topped tracked prime movers hauled the big guns up nearly vertical bypass routes. The scars showed what a great part planes and artillery played in this mountain battle. The Japs defended every bit of the road--but lost. The last big fight was at Irisan, just before the city limits. Here was a wrecked Jap tank. As it grew dark I decided to find a place to stay. Who should I find but Harry Blajin and the boys camped out in a hillside, tents staked on a dry rice paddy. They were all in sweaters and complained slightly of being frozen. Their PX supplies had just arrived, so we had a pleasant evening comparing notes and occasionally being lifted slightly off the ground by a big gun banking away just behind the tent, or listening to another infiltration being taken care of a few hundred yards away. Conrad was tented a short distance from Harry's place. Ever since the 37th got into the fight at the foot of the mountains the Japs have been moving backward.

Next morning we had flap jacks and coffee, and then climbed into a jeep for a short trip into town on a road jammed with vehicles of all kinds. A sign at the cemetery advises Blackout Here-Curfew 7pm-7am-Do not impede military traffic. Here the last battle for Baguio was fought. We rounded the corner to see a scene of destruction. At the corner of Bokowkan Road and Naguilian Road a lone statue stood bolt upright with one hand raised. It was a stiff, blackened Jap who didn't retreat fast enough. We went down to the house where the folks lived. On the front porch I found the souvenir Betty wanted, a Jap steel helmet. Its owner was nearby but was in no condition to protest the appropriation. The building had been smashed by a hit. A long tunnel filled with captured (1942) U.S. ammunition ran into the hill behind. Bulldozers were clearing the streets as we turned up Trinidad road past the undamaged Church of the Resurrection and into the completely wrecked Market area. The ground was cratered. Some buildings had vanished entirely, although part of the Palace Hotel stands. Eschbach's church was merely four walls. We looked at the South Drive house, which was loose in the joints from a bomb which hit just outside but otherwise o.k. Some German's furniture was still partially intact. Finally we arrived at Navy Road, detouring the blown Teacher's Camp bridge. "Jimmy!" someone called. It was one of the McCann girls. "Your mother is with Captain Keith," she said. I hurried down the hillside. There she was, thin and shaken and tearful but alive and undamaged.

She had been taken in by the chief and Lura after Notre Dame was bombed, along with Mrs. Saleeby and Muzzie Whitmarsh. The Keiths were good to them and furnished food when food was not to be had. (Chief says a Jap soldier fainted in front of his house during the retreat and was beheaded by his officer.) During the last few days, when shelling grew heavy. Mother decided to go further out, and stayed in an Igorot Village below Mines View park. She returned the day before I arrived after nearly being hit by a stray shell. She's been through hell.

Mrs. Saleevy had an injured shoulder but was as keen in mind as ever. Muzzie is quite deaf but cheerful. Mother says she didn't wear well. A short time later Russ Brines of AP arrived. We went to the telephone building, where a PCAU unit was distributing food, and secured rations, which when added to the cheese and figs I'd brought up made a good meal. Mother's digestion is in typical pre beri-beri conditions and her feet are swollen slightly, but vitamins will fix that. At the church where 7000 people had sought refuge, I found the sick lying on improvised beds made from two pews. Many were praying at the altar rail, some for deliverance, some for safety for their families yet unheard from. Dr. Handel was caring for the refugees. Among many people I saw were the Pastor, Miguel Prez-Rubio, the Tuscheffs, and others. A photographer from Yank magazine was busy (if you can get copies of Yank you'll have a good report of the war here.) Russ and I had lunch with Fredericks and his staff on Quezon Hill while waiting for some kind of word on transportation for the ladies to Manila. Joe Rice lived downstairs; if anything he looks more Joe Rice than ever. It was an honor to lunch with the commander of the regiment that has been the first on so many occasions--and may be first into Tokyo. I thanked him for rescuing so many of us, both at Bilibid and Baguio. Back at Keith's we met a man named Villaluz who ran the city's water testing laboratory. In his house was stored a good deal of Mother's and my belongings, including her inlaid chairs and dresser (beds were burned elsewhere), some of my books, photo albums, electric stove and my Contax. All around the house bombs and shells had fallen. The Villaluz's had stayed in an air raid shelter for weeks. The road to his house through the little valley behind Brent is lined with caves stuffed with medical supplies and ammunition, some burned, some intact. I hitched a ride on three vehicles, including an ambulance, a jeep, and an armored car. Late that afternoon Jim Bell showed up. He had come to Baguio on business, had found his brother David, verified the death of his mother from dysentery March 30 at a house in Buisad, taken David to Manila in a Cub, then returned to get his jeep and to look us up. And Peachy came in (Dr. Stafford and wife had been found at Speth's by his son Dr. Charles, an Army captain.) She brought apples and magazines. We spent Tuesday night there. The guns echoed through the draws as they fired at distant Nip positions. We've got everything up there from rifles right on up to the biggest thing that moves—Li'l Abner. The ladies were nervous when the guns fired--and I can't blame them. Time after time they escaped being killed by a few yards. It was dark and eerie in Baguio.

Wednesday morning Jim went out to Demonstration by himself on a one man reconnaissance gut found nothing except a bomb-damaged mill and intact shaft-house. Beguet and Balatoc were reportedly wrecked as was Itogon, by bombing. Then we returned and took us out to check on various people and houses. Dona Rosa de Zabaljaurequi was ok but several members of her family were missing and one of her houses is gone. Mrs. Lenze was staying with her. Gusti was quite sick. Jim found some of his things with the Penas. We drove about and found these things: Florence Hearald's house ok, guest house burned, office bombed, strafed. Country Club main building, annex ok,sports pav. partly wrecked, some cottages ok. Baguio hospital wrecked thoroughly, Notre Dame burned, bombed beyond recognition. Brent School all ok after use by Jâp's as a hospital.
Teachers Camp mostly damaged but many cottages ok. Staplers house ok, ditto Crouter, Van Schaicks, NBC house, Craig's, Elser's, Speth's, Keith's. Muller's, Blasted; City Hall, Zigzag, Pines, Government Center, #31 Engineer Hill, BPW office, Lopez Bldg., everything else on Session Road except phone ex, part of Palace Hotel, bldg. next to phone ex. Church damaged slightly. Whitmarsh apartments, house gone. Phil's house damaged but not badly. When a bomb hits anywhere near a frame building it pulls the boards loose, throws fragments through the roof and sides, and makes the place look a wreck--but actually, many of these places can be repaired with a little hammering. And as the Army moves in it does a lot of repairing. You've seen that. I think Baguio will be on its feet again long before Manila is completely repaired. The pines are burned with napalm at many places,

but the majority of trees are not in bad shape.
There are no lights and no water yet.

I did not want to take Mother to Manila in a jeep
and she wanted to stay a few more days to get in
touch with various people in town. So I left Peachy
to arrange transportation for all three and began
working at this end to help them out. Santo Tomas
repatriation office advises that a ship will leave in
two or three weeks. I hope to put Mother into the
hospital here for a rest, then send her on the boat.
She needs a long rest. Hogan's Alley was a typical
Baguio scene. Half the buildings were damaged by
bomb fragments. The sala was littered with dirty
mats and spoiling rice. Jim poked his .45 in the
doorways after kicking them open. In one we
round some Jap language handbooks. Another had
a few pieces of stationery from the Mitsui Mining
Company. The third contained the sprawling body
of a surprised Jap, whose blood stained the floor.
He had been dead several days.

Jim and I left Baguio after lunch and had an
uneventful, pleasant trip down to Manila, not liking
the wave of heat that came at us when we hit the
lowlands. Everywhere is the Army, everywhere the
spreading might of the United States. We had raisin
bread-roast beef sandwiches at 1corps hq., then
sped on in the gathering night, reaching Manila at
9:30 last night. I found the office this morning a
beehive of activity with news flashes pouring in. It
was a good thing I'd returned when I did.
I have some of Dad's records, including a list of
stock certificates in his possession which were later
burned.

Jim
Please circulate this letter among Baguio people
when you see them.

One of the intriguing stories to come out of the last days of our internment and liberation was the rescue of the Los Banos Camp. Carl Widdoes, the son of "Ma and Pa Widdoes," (beloved missionaries stationed at San Fernando) had been interned with us but later moved to the remote Los Banos Camp. One of the top U.S. ranking officers, an OS Alumnus, in Manila cabled Carl to win a certain football game for him. Carl replied that he would, if the officer could locate his parents. He knew the Manila group had been liberated, but had received no word from his parents. The officer immediately inquired about them and tracked them to the Los Banos Camp.

Los Banos was south of us across a large lake. They were very isolated and in dire circumstances. A woman from that camp that I met on the boat going home, said that they were chewing on grasses and leaves for extra nourishment. Rescue was difficult because of the isolation, but the resourcefulness of the American forces was not to be thwarted. They studied the daily movement of the guards. Each morning the Japanese soldiers gathered in one spot to exercise, putting aside their weapons to do so. So one early morning our Am-traks raced across the lake. At the same time planes over head dropped men by parachutes into the camp. Killing the unarmed guards, they quickly guided the internees to the Am-traks for a lengthy dash across the lakes to the newly built Bilibid Prison. This entire miraculous rescue was due to the timely correspondence of a football coach and an Army officer concerning a game. If there had not been that feeling of urgency between the two, the rescue would not have been so prompt and may not have ended so satisfactory.

Chapter 32
Life began to reassemble...

After our dramatic rescue by the 37th Infantry and 1st Cavalry, our days were marked by visits from homesick GIs, health checks for each of us by Army doctors, and the issuance of GI clothing and Red Cross supplies,. We were able to write letters home via the Red Cross. We cooked extra goodies from generous GI rations in addition to the food the Army prepared for us. There is one "telling" picture by an Army photographer of a group of us in Bilibid gaping in wonder at a truck full of freshly baked bread. It was overwhelming to see and reminded me of the story of those with Jesus when three loaves of bread fed hundreds.

The main conversation revolved around the day when we would finally go home. Life continued on. A new baby was born. Some seriously ill were taken to an Army hospital for better care. Life began to reassemble into a new rhythm of the joy of having been rescued and alive, along with a deep hurt as the growing count of casualties was brought to us daily. The cost was untold, the horrors hard to imagine.

"War is hell" barely describes the suffering, death, destruction, and calamities that fell to the residents of Manila. Today, some fifty years later, the losses of friends and families are still being felt. Multiply that by all the ensuing wars of Korea, Vietnam, Cambodia, the Gulf War, Bosnia, Israel and Palestine and we have a damning tragic picture of the 20th century. May the dawning of a new century bring to us, the sense to oppose war. We must convey, not only to world powers but also to our friends, children and grandchildren, that "without a vision, we perish." Reporters speak glibly of the next war as though it is inevitable. It may be necessary to hit the streets in protest, just as in the sixties. This must be a global cause with people united for peace. Perhaps a futile dream, but one we must cling to and espouse before all other causes.

Churches must make that cause clear or we will become a people without a message.

Finally, in March, 1945, plans began to unfold for our return to America. The method used to decide who was to go and when was by the drawing of names. Bessie Crim's name was in the first group. As we all gathered on the steps of the prison to bid her farewell, there were tears, laughter and promises to see each other in the States.

For Carol, this was the first time she had experienced anyone leaving Camp for as a rule, in the three years most of us really did not think seriously of leaving. Being in jail her entire life did not lend itself to farewells, but she sensed we were going through big changes. As Ed held her and she hugged Bessie, she started to cry with her tears flowing down Ed's bare back. "Going away" was beyond her knowledge but she knew this was a "big deal." In the past few months these young kids had undergone changes, moves, and frightening scenes of fire and warfare and now this strange breaking of ties. Until this day, Carol cannot say good bye to people without the same kind of "deluge."

Three years of internment left adults also with strange idiosyncrasies. One of mine is not being able to throw away a nice box. I hoard them in the top of the closets or under the bed until Ed decrees some of the collection must go. The urge to hoard is still strong. Several days ago we were in a J.C. Penny's store, which was being renovated. As we entered, a man with a load of torn-out, nicely finished wood was exiting the store in order to dump it. My one thought was "Golly, that wood would sure make some nice shelves!" Of course my next thought was "Helen, get a life!" But in America the waste of useful things which others, could use is so evident. Perhaps we do need to keep emphasizing more recycling of all kinds. I remember a story during the war on the mayor of Amsterdam talking to the mayor of New York on a visit here. The New York mayor asked what he could do to help Amsterdam, and their mayor answered, "Just send us the garbage you throw away each day!"

Finally, our names were drawn and we received word that a contingent of us would fly to Leyte to wait for a ship to take us home. As anxious as we all were to leave the confines of internment, we were losing a way of life that had developed around loss, fear, and the art of improvising creatively and doing without. None of us felt much remorse to say "good bye" to such days, months and years.

Yet in the years to come, those ties and experiences were deeper and more meaningful than most. Our "get-togethers", though getting scarcer as the years go by, are rife with laughter as well as tears of remembrance. We had found new values, new insights and a deeper reverence for life. A new respect for friends and foes alike had developed as we found deep within all of us a universal humanity. To this day we "think the thoughts and speak the talk" of those three long years of internment.

On March 15 we left the destroyed city of Manila, the former "Pearl of the Orient." It was now a city full of jeeps, tanks, U.S. military, and Filipinos trying to get back some sense of normalcy amid devastating ruins. Some estimated it would be 40 years before Manila would be rebuilt. Sheer doggedness allowed for its quick reconstruction, though never to its former splendor. Certainly it began to function as a city sooner than anyone expected. I do not think stateside people were really aware of the terrible condition of the city. When I visited Harrisburg, Pennsylvania to get a U.S. birth certificate for Carol, the clerk over the loud speaker asked a dumb bureaucrat how he should do this. The man from an inner office shouted back, "Why didn't she go to City Hall in Manila and get one before she left?" I had to reply with some asperity, "The city lies in ruins!"

Our group, after more farewells, was driven through a destroyed city to Nichols Airfield. There we met an equally jubilant group of officers who were also bound for home. It was the first time in three years that they were given a furlough. We talked and visited until the planes taxied down the hastily restored runway. We were all to fly to Leyte. Those in charge insisted that the internees go on the first two planes, the officers following on the third one. We were to fly over still enemy-held territory and were given "Mae West" vests to wear in case we were shot down and crashed into the sea. The plane was a C47, a cargo plane with metal bucket seats running the length of the plane on both sides. In spite of discomfort and forebodings as to a safe trip, we soared off into the blue sky with exhalation and a sense of freedom we had not had for a long time. Soon the pilot sent a message that he wanted each of us to have a turn sitting in the cockpit with him. As we flew over Corregidor, it was mine and Carol's turn. It was sobering to look down on the tiny former stronghold of the American Army where so much bravery, suffering, and heart-breaking defeat had taken place. The suffering and death those men and women knew would be our Filipino "days of infamy" to remember forever.

In a seemingly short time, we landed on the newly-laid tarmac at Tacloban, where we were greeted by Army people who organized us to be taken to our own unknown destination. They kept the men in Tacloban and drove us to a convalescent hospital on a beach some miles from there. All during the war, the Japanese (though separating us most of the time) at least kept us in the same area where we could see each other every day. Here were our own Americans separating us at a very emotional time. I'm sure that they had their reasons, but we were surprised and annoyed to be separated. The beach where the hospital was located was lovely, a wonderful treat to see blue seas, blue skies, and be free. There were countless tents, where men from the Battle of Leyte and other places were recuperating. Some of them said, "They're just getting us fit to invade Japan!" We were to be there until sometime in April, about a six week duration.

A female nurse took charge of the women. She haughtily ordered us to line up. Rather aggressively, she loaded us in jeeps and we started off with a roar of engines, down unpaved, bumpy roads. We were really puzzled by her confrontational attitude. The next day she was equally vexed when she saw how the GIs had angled the partition door to our assigned shower. They had, with motives afore thought, maneuvered the door into place so that they could, on passing casually by, get a glimpse of us showering. That little scheme really set her off. She was so angry that she alone ripped the doorposts out of the ground and positioned them so those scheming GIs could no longer glimpse our skinny internment bodies! Soon afterward we learned that she had had a complete breakdown due to the long duration of her stay in the South Pacific. To be in charge of a group of freedom happy "dames" from the South Pacific internment was her breaking point. The effect of those in combatant situations can last a lifetime, and I often wonder how or if she recovered.

An extremely horrifying bit of news came to us on the night of our arrival on Leyte. The last plane leaving Manila with those wonderful officers aboard crashed into a mountain on Leyte as they came into land. It was in Japanese territory, and they all perished.

A happier experience involved another nurse, Romaine, with whom we kept in contact after the war. Carol, upon having food different from the usual rice and camotes, did not relish the plentiful food provided by the Army. Upon arriving on Leyte, she practically refused to eat. The nurse was concerned and speculated that perhaps she missed having rice. So each day she cooked a bowl full of rice. Lo, and behold, that internment camp kid downed it with gusto and then started to eat the food served by the Army. That wonderful nurse cooked her rice every day until the time we sailed for home.

Come to think of it, all she had until we returned home from the Philippines had been Army food, from two nations, bad and indifferent. She did not like sweet things since we did not have an oversupply of sugar and only occasionally were able to splurge. She was home over a year before she consumed a complete ice cream cone. I never could say, "Well, if you don't eat your dinner there will be no desert" for she did not really care.

Thoughtfulness was again given to us by a Navy man. He was ashore on Leyte with his camera roaming the beach. He struck up a conversation with me, and offered to leave his camera for a day so that we could take pictures of Carol and the other children. He returned the next day, and retrieved the camera and film. He had it developed aboard ship and came ashore to give us treasured pictures of which heretofore we only had one or two.

Each day, we were constantly bombarded and overwhelmed with such kindnesses. The children were

overwhelmed with attention, for these men and women had
not seen American kids for a long time, just like the group
that drove us out of Manila at the time of the fire. One day
an officer came and said he wanted all the kids in the nine-
to-twelve-age group. The officers wanted to take them to a
party! Such excitement as he "jeeped" off the kids the next
morning! Their parents were expecting them back in the
afternoon. They did not return until midnight. The kids
were hilariously overcome with gifts of silk parachutes,
major maple leaf pins, badges, caps and anything else
those loving guys could give them that was not nailed down
at officers headquarter.

In the meantime, from the day of our arrival until our
departure, the internee women were not neglected. We
visited with GIs constantly on the beach. They talked of
families at home, showed us pictures, and confided in us.
One day one of them was talking to several of us. He said
to meet him on the beach at eight o'clock that night. We
were all there when he arrived with a huge hamper of all
kinds of food. He plunked it down on the sand and said,
"Now, eat!" And, believe me, we did!

One day Win Smith came to me and told several of us
to be ready to go to a party on the Flagship of Admiral
Nimitz. Alas, I could not go as Carol was still not eating
and I could not in good conscience leave her. They all had
a great party. The biggest adventure for them was climbing
up the side of this immense ship by a rope ladder.

One memorable day, Lucy and Jack Vinson, Bunny and
Wayne Miller, and Ed and I got to ride into Tacloban where
the men still were stationed. I think they were a bit jealous
of the attention we were receiving from the hordes of GIs
surrounding us. In fact, they started to thumb a ride to
our camp almost every day. A year or so later at Juniata
College, a former enlisted man came up to Ed, and asked if
he had ever been on the island of Leyte. Of course, Ed
said, "Yes!" He replied, "Well, you hitched a ride with me
on my jeep from Tacloban to the hospital site!"

As the six of us were "sightseeing" on the wharf in
Tacloban, a Seabee from Samar talked to us and invited us
to come with him on the small boat to Samar. Since there
were only men there, we girls wondered where we would

find a restroom. Well, we were in luck because as we neared the shore, there was a long jetty built at the end of it. On top of the roof was a large banner on which was printed "Girls, here it is!" The night before, they had had a party for the nurses from Leyte, and had thoughtfully provided a "powder room." Since the sign was still up, we claimed it as our own.

As we came ashore our host said, "I'll introduce you to the chaplain and he'll show you around." Well, the chaplain had been to the party, too, and the island resounded with the snores of recuperating Seabees. Our host told us to make ourselves at home as he had work to do. He said we were free to go anyplace we wanted and to make ourselves at home until someone woke up.

We had just started to stroll down the beautiful, tropical beach when an enraged shore patrol demanded to know who we were. When Wayne answered in his haughty Harvard accent, he was answered by the shore patrol with hot vehemence. He said that we women were in dire danger of being raped, and painted a picture of all the Seabees ready to pantingly grab us. Skinny as we were in an assortment of GI clothing and Red Cross stuff, I'm sure they would have had second thoughts. The Seabees' patrol ordered us in no uncertain terms to get off the beach. We forlornly wandered up to the impressive frame housing the Seabees had built for themselves. I think if he had had the right he would have put us in the "Clink," but then we were accustomed to that, too.

By this time, the chaplain was awake and others were stirring about. They were outraged at the stupid attitude of the shore patrol and so endeavored to out-do themselves in showing us a good time and giving us the welcome of our lives. First, they took us to a boxing match, where Bunny had the honor of awarding the cup to the winner. They took us to lunch where we were overwhelmed with the really good food. They showed us the bakery with rows and rows of freshly baked Philadelphia cinnamon sticky buns, nuts and all. They tasted so wonderful after years of weevils and rice. They also took us to the officers' outdoor recreation area, where they proudly served us ice cold beer, the first iced drink we'd had in over three years.

159

The Seabees are surely the arm of the services to choose. They come in shortly after an invasion and rebuild the area to serve the Army. They were so cordial that they suggested it was foolish to return to Leyte, when we could be with them until our ship arrived. It was very tempting, but not acceptable to those in charge of us so we dutifully sailed back to Leyte with an amazing new definition of hospitality.

We went to shore, only to be met by a GI officer who was outraged at our appearance as he thought we were "Army" and dressed in a shocking manner. He also included Jim Thompson who had happened by. Our men were bawled out in true military terms for being out of uniform. He asked us why we looked such a mess. Finally, after the tirade ceased, the men identified themselves and quieted the poor man down. We told him we were L.Ps--the label given us when we arrived on Leyte, meaning Liberated Personnel.

As we anxiously waited for "our ship to come in," life went on, friendships formed, and we again adapted to new surroundings. For the most part, this time was a happy, outgoing experience. Finally, our names were called. Quite a few of us were informed we were to leave the next day on a small Dutch lend-lease ship. Our stay at the First Convalescent Hospital on a Leyte beach was at an end. Again, we repacked and discarded, on our way (again) to a new experience.

This time on a homeward bound ship, 800 feet long, packed with exultant GIs and relieved, happy internees. Due to Japanese ships and submarines, this journey lasted for three weeks, zigzagging across the Pacific. No lights were allowed to show and garbage was dumped in darkness so that it would not be seen. The first night on board the ship we did not sail. Most of us sat on deck, watching a sentimental propaganda movie called "To Russia with Love." It was made for the purpose of furthering good relations with Russia at that particular time. Under the usual star-lit night, we heard a classical number used as a theme tune throughout the movies. It was beautiful then, and whenever I hear it now I'm instantly back on that ship, exalting in freedom and new hope for life after three years of grueling internment.

The United States officers who manned the ship under a Dutch captain, voluntarily gave women with small children their very comfortable quarters. The remaining internees were allotted bunks below deck. Jessie Junkin, Billy (her three year old son), Carol and I were assigned a state room. The doors had been removed throughout the ship because if struck, the doors could jam and the occupants would have a problem getting out. So instead, curtains hung over each door.

For some reason, our door did not have a curtain. After living publicly for three years, this should not have bothered us, but we were pretty envious of those having curtains. There was much coming and going in the corridors and we wished that we had a curtain. After we settled in, Ed came up to see our "luxurious" quarters. As we entered, there was a uniformed man on his hands and knees examining a slightly leaky pipe under one of the bunks. I thought, "Here's my chance to see about a curtain." As he rose muttering about Americans ruining the ship, I asked very politely about the possibility of a curtain for our door. His response was to stomp out in a real temper. Ed turned to me and said, "Do you know who that was? That was the captain of the ship!" Oh, well, I tried, dumb as I was about rank and uniforms. Of course we were curtain-less for the rest of the trip.

The soldiers going home played with our children constantly. One young man, a lawyer from New York, was really fond of Carol. He would play with her but when he tired, he'd rub the top of her head and say, "You better go back to your mother. There's a point growing on the top of your head!" He shared some of his childhood with us. His parents divorced and his father married again, a woman with several children of her own. They lived in a penthouse overlooking the city of New York. To control their wild brood, they put bars at all the windows in the kids' area and that is how he grew up with a wild easy-going bunch of kids. He was obviously a happy-go-lucky kind of person. Carol loved every minute she spent with him. I often wonder what happened to him.

We carried life preservers with us at all times in case of an attack and possible sinking. This was a bit of a drag, literally, as they were fairly heavy and bulky. One of Carol's remarks about the ocean spray caused by the on-rushing ship was "Look at all those soap suds!" Soap, being scarce in camp, she was very impressed.

Another remark I also remember with some pain. Dr. Lloyd Cunningham said that he had not expected to see Ed come home with us as he had been so sick from the food and intestinal problems in camp. So, we Angenys were a very grateful threesome as we zigged and zagged across the Pacific. Fortunately, for us, it lived up to its name. The other peacefulness was that the Japanese Navy did not get us in their sights.

As we plowed through the ocean, we found out we were to see Honolulu. Surely, surely, we thought they would dock and give us all a short stay for relief from the long voyage but that was not to be. We sailed right by Diamond Head. As we passed by Honolulu, a small plane whizzed by our ship, returned, and flew very low between our two smoke stacks which really rattled our teeth. We never knew if it was a bored pilot or he knew that the ship was filled with furloughed soldiers and internees.

The day before we docked in San Francisco, the officers had the crew bring out voluminous supplies of food not consumed on the trip. These supplies were to be dumped overboard at night. They did not want to arrive in San Francisco with food as it would cut down on how the ship would be supplied on its trip back. This really amazed those of us who had just gotten off starvation rations and had left a place where there was lack of food. War causes mixed emotions at strange regulations and unbelievable waste of many resources. There were cans of lemon powder. One of the crew told us they used it to scrub the decks as it bleached the wood. There were crates of soda crackers and other food stuffs. We internees started to open the crackers and eat them with relish as crackers had been unknown to us for three years. At that point, the GIs came, too, and we had great cracker feast before all were dumped that night.

162

There was a Japanese sub scare off the coast of California, so we felt quite victorious the next day as we sailed under the glorious, beautiful Golden Gate Bridge. We were on deck in tears, cheering as we had our first glimpse of our homeland. Lloyd Cunningham had been told by the Captain that we were to clean up our spaces before we left the ship. So poor Lloyd was running around fruitlessly trying to convince us to go to our cabins and do our bidden duty. He was a most frustrated man as we all ignored him and waited breathlessly to dock.

But when we did so, FBI men came aboard to question us and collect any diaries we might have written. Any personal record that we had of the past three years, and held on to at great risk, was taken from us with a promise of a quick return. Ed had only a few pages, but Natalie Crouter had a complete diary of each day spent in camp. She was devastated when she had to hand her account over to the FBI. Her notes were lost by the FBI for some time. Months later they were found in a storage building in Kansas City. Later she wrote the book Forbidden Diary using her notes. It is a most complete account of our internment days.

After being questioned, we were permitted to go ashore. There, the Red Cross met us with "ditty bags" of toilet supplies and vouchers for new clothing and the trip home. The pastor from the San Francisco Church of the Brethren met us and generously took us to their home where we stayed for several days. They took us shopping and showed us parts of the city. It was exhilarating to shop for new clothes, shedding our GI stuff as we bought new things to replace them. For panties, I had been wearing camouflaged GI shorts. It was a happy day for me when I could discard them. Previously, I had explained to Carol about people living in individual homes and having a separate room called the dining room which was just used for eating. As soon as she entered the Gnag's home she asked, "Where is the dining room?" Another new oddity to her was women wearing hosiery. One day in the post office standing at the counter, I felt something edging its way up the seam of my hose. It was Carol, tracing with her finger, the raised edge of the seam, completely puzzled.

So, life began again as we once knew it. Even with war shortages in the U.S. at the time, people looked more prosperous than when we left in 1940. We were given ration stamps for shoes and other things. We were enamored at the prosperity we saw because of higher wages and more jobs.

We had arrived in May and by the end of August the war was over. On August 6, Ed's birthday, the atomic bomb was dropped and not long after that peace was declared. That day we went to downtown Philadelphia and with thousands of others celebrated peace at last. New hopes and new plans filled our lives as they did the world over.

Recently I heard Elie Weisel on Charley Rose's talk show on PBS discussing the War and the Holocaust. They talked of the indignities human beings had inflicted upon one another in this century. Charley said, "Well, do you now consider yourself to be 'the voice' to the world about these things?" Weisel answered, "No, because it must be everyone's voice!"

As this tale comes to a close, we can only hope that you, our children, grandchildren and great-grandchildren down through the ages will always be a voice raised in love and indignation for the right of all humanity. We pray that this will be your witness to God's Kingdom on earth...

Acknowledgments

Publishing my mom's memoir has been a real privilege and it would not have happened except for the encouragement of various people. Thanks to my writing group especially Debi K., to history teacher Greg G., to author Sandi Sumner, to friend Gail S., to my husband Harry, and to my sister Carol who graces the cover of this book as #205.

All proceeds of this book will be donated to Heifer International, an organization founded by Dan West, a member of the Church of the Brethren. As a family, we knew him and have been involved with this hunger project for years. These contributions can be one way we can be "a voice raised in love...for the right of all humanity."

Yes, Mom, you may now "rest in peace."

Phyllis Angeny Hochstetler

Helen & Carol.